Historic
Racing Car
Models

Historic Racing Car Models

THEIR STORIES AND HOW TO MAKE THEM

Frank Ross, Jr.

Illustrated with diagrams and photos

Lothrop, Lee & Shepard Company • New York

A Division of William Morrow & Company, Inc.

Photos of the racing car models by George A. Haddad

1 2 3 4 5 80 79 78 77 76

Library of Congress Cataloging in Publication Data

Ross, Frank Xavier, (date)
  Historic racing car models.

  Bibliography: p.
  SUMMARY: Stories of six famous racing cars, from 1895 to the 1970's, and
detailed directions for making models of the vehicles.
  1. Automobiles, Racing—Models—Juvenile literature. [1. Automobiles, Racing—
Models. 2. Models and modelmaking] I. Title.
TL237.R67   629.22'1'8   76-41168
ISBN 0-688-41770-1
ISBN 0-688-51770-6 lib. bdg.

Other Books by Frank Ross, Jr.

Contents

For my dearest *Laura*

Introduction

Racing cars and car races originated in France in the late nineteenth century. At that time France was a beehive of activity in developing and promoting the automobile, a new but mechanically primitive means of transport. The first motor car race was held in 1894. It was an open-road contest from Paris to Rouen, a distance of some eighty miles. The competition was sponsored by a Paris newspaper whose editor saw news value in having cars race against one another. He was right. The sport caught on quickly in France and in a few years had spread to Germany, Italy, Belgium, and even far-off America.

Car racing on the open road was a particular favorite of the French. In the years following the Paris–Rouen contest many others were organized, such as the Paris–Bordeaux–Paris race of 1895; the Paris–Berlin contest of 1901, first long-distance international race; the grueling Paris–Vienna race held in 1902; and the Paris–Madrid competition of 1903.

Aside from the great excitement these races aroused, they were extremely dangerous, both to drivers and spectators. Drivers careening along public roads, desperately trying to avoid animals and people, inevitably caused casualties. Cars suffered mechanical breakdowns and blown tires, and often catapulted off the road against trees or other obstacles, and into the crowd of spectators. At the end of almost every road race there was a list of injured and dead.

Because of the shocking casualties, especially in the Paris–Madrid race, road racing was banned in France for several years. However, after much pressure from racing enthusiasts and automobile manufacturers, French authorities relented and granted permission for these road contests to resume under the strictest regulations. First of the road races to be conducted again was at Le Mans, in 1906. It set the standards for the Grand Prix races that came later and are now considered the super contests of the car-racing world.

Some of the famous Grand Prix races that are held throughout the world in the course of the year are the Le Mans, in France; Nürburgring, West Germany; Monte Carlo, Monaco; and the Watkins Glen Grand Prix in the United States.

In the United States, car racing took a different direction. The sport became popular on closed tracks, mainly because authorities frowned on the use of public roads for such a highly dangerous activity. The most famous of the closed track races in the United States is the Indianapolis 500, first run in 1911. Every Memorial Day weekend this super car-racing spectacle draws some of the best drivers in the world; attracts more than 200,000 spectators; and offers the winning driver the biggest prize in car racing, over $250,000.

In the early years of auto racing, there was little if any difference between racing cars and those used by the general public. However, by the early decades of the 1900s the situation changed. Cars were designed and built just for racing. They no longer looked like the cars for general use and they were much faster and more powerful. Drivers of these cars required exceptional stamina, strength, and reflexes. Many of these racing specialists became famous: Christian Lautenschlager, Camille Jenatzy, and Barney Oldfield among the real old-timers, and Juan Manuel Fangio, Stirling Moss, and Graham Hill among the modern stars.

When early automobile manufacturers saw the great public interest aroused by racing, they became eager participants. If a particular builder's car became the victor, it meant fame and a vigorous boost in business. So in the effort to build the best racing car, new mechanical features were developed to make engines more powerful, to increase speed, to improve steering and braking, and, not least important, to make tires stronger and less likely to blow out. If these mechanical improvements proved successful in the rough, grueling arena of racing, especially open-road competitions, they were eventually built into the cars sold to the public. Thus, aside from sporting thrills, racing cars have made a constructive contribution to the overall advancement of the automobile.

This book tells briefly the stories of a few of the more famous racing cars, past and present. Included are the Panhard-Levassor, one of the earliest cars and winner of the Paris–Bordeaux–Paris race of 1895; the powerful Mercedes, scourge of road races in Europe and America in the early 1900s; the graceful Duesenberg, first American racing car to win a European competition; the Maserati, one of the first and best of the modern racers; the Lotus-Ford that flashed with dazzling brilliance in European and American races; and finally, the McLaren M16 that helped to introduce the present new breed of landbound thunderbolts. Each added its bit to the story of the racing car's evolution from the earliest years to the current era.

But this is primarily a craft book; in addition to the stories of these racing cars, it provides detailed directions, diagrams, and photos for making models of the vehicles. This is a fascinating and enjoyable activity. If you have never seen any of the racing cars mentioned above, the colorful, completed models will give you a far better idea of what they were like than any number of words or pictures can. The end results will be surprisingly realistic, and will give you a feeling of satisfaction and accomplishment, even if they are not 100 percent perfect. Finally, the models make interesting decorations for your room and will serve as conversation pieces with family and friends.

Materials and Tools

When making your models, work on a sturdy table with a flat smooth surface. Cover the work surface with paper, preferably light-colored. A sheet of oaktag is good. This can be bought at many stationery stores and art supply shops. The paper covering will protect the table top from glue spills and accidental knife scratches. Also, the light color of the paper will help you spot tools and materials which may become mixed up as you work on a model.

Make sure the work table is one you can use continuously over a period of time. It is an awful bother to have to put away tools and materials after every work session.

The following is a list of the materials and tools you will need to make the models in this book.

Construction paper

Construction paper and rigid cardboard are almost the only kinds of paper needed to build the racing-car models described in the chapters ahead. Get the kind of construction paper that is used in school for art class projects. It is recommended for making these models because it comes in a variety of colors, bends easily, and takes gluing very well. It also gives your finished models a better look than pieces of scrap paper would. Paint shops selling art supplies, stationery stores, and hobby or craft shops are all good sources for buying construction paper at a reasonable price.

Rigid cardboard

If you have any empty shoe boxes at home, they will give you the rigid cardboard you need. Empty cereal boxes, while not as rigid as shoe boxes, may also be used. Two or three pieces glued together will make thicker cardboard that is rigid enough to use.

A box made of several layers of compressed paper, like a cigar box, is excellent for parts like wheels and chassis. The owner of a store where cigars are sold may be happy to let you have all his empty boxes; you would be helping him solve his waste disposal problem.

Rigid cardboard may also be bought in sheets. An inexpensive kind, easy to draw on and cut, is matting board. This is commonly used for framing pictures. Art stores and some camera supply shops carry it.

When choosing your rigid cardboard, make sure it does not have a shiny surface. A slick surface will prevent glue from sticking properly. Also, drawing on it with pen and ink or crayon will be difficult.

Cardboard cylinders

You will need cardboard cylinders for making the wheels on the more modern racing-car models. Use the cylinders from rolls of paper toweling, waxed paper, aluminum foil, or plastic wrap. If you can't find these, cylinders from rolls of toilet tissue may be substituted. However, the larger cylinders are better because they are stiffer.

Drinking straws

Drinking straws are the last of the paper materials for building the racing-car models. The large or jumbo size straws are best. You may have these in your home. If you must buy them, look for the plainest straws you can find. Too much decoration on the straws will make your finished models less attractive.

Wood

Wooden matchsticks and round toothpicks are the only wood materials needed for the models. The matchsticks should be the extra long kind commonly used for lighting fires in fireplaces. These may be bought in most hardware stores. Just make sure to remove the flammable tips before you work with them. The matchstick wood is needed to make axles and steering columns.

Round toothpicks are needed to make brake handles, lamp decorations, and crank handles for your models. For the most part, only the thick center portion of a toothpick is used. Be sure to get the round kind, not flat ones.

Hammer

While you may need a hammer only occasionally, it is useful to have a light one available, if one can be spared from the family toolbox. A hammer is useful for tapping the back of a knife when cutting wooden matchsticks or toothpicks.

String

A 12-inch length of white, medium-thick string is needed for the sprocket chains of the Mercedes model.

Pipe cleaners

Flexible pipe cleaners are needed for making safety roll bars on some of the models.

India ink, crayon, poster paints, and aluminum paint

These are needed to draw designs on the wheels and bodies of the cars and also to color various parts.

Pencils

A medium soft (No. 2½) and a soft (No. 2) pencil will be helpful for measuring and drawing the various parts of the models.

Compass

Many circles will have to be drawn and cut for the racing-car models. A good compass is therefore essential.

Ruler

A 12-inch ruler for making measurements on your construction paper and checking those on the diagrams in the book will be necessary throughout the building of the models.

Scissors

A strong, sharp scissors is needed for cutting construction paper and cardboard parts. A small straight cuticle scissors is also helpful for cutting away excess paper from small and complex parts.

Knife

Next to the scissors, a sharp knife is the most important tool for building the models. It is necessary for cutting the lengths and angles of the various wooden parts. The point of the knife is also used for scoring the construction paper. This means running the tip of the knife once or twice along the dotted line to be folded. Scoring will give the paper a straighter, cleaner fold.

Any small knife with a reasonably good point and cutting edge will do. An X-acto knife, made especially for model-making and art work, is excellent. However, care must be taken when scoring paper with it. Because it is so sharp, too much pressure can easily cut the paper rather than make a scored line.

Tweezers

Unless your fingers are quite nimble for holding small pieces, tweezers are a must.

Drawing pen

Use a pen with black ink for drawing designs on the models. A black felt Flair pen, or a similar make, may be substituted.

Glue

Elmer's Glue-All and Sobo glue are both excellent for attaching the various parts of the car models. Both dry quickly and have good sticking qualities. A 4-ounce bottle of either kind is enough to make all the models.

Masking tape

Pieces of masking tape are needed for holding your construction paper to the work table as you draw the patterns or designs.

Nail

A nail is needed for making holes in various parts of the models.

Block of wood

A small block of wood will be helpful as a support when matchsticks or toothpicks are being cut.

General Directions

The six racing-car models in this book are presented in chronological order. They show some of the ways in which racing cars have changed over the past three quarters of a century. The cars and their dates are as follows:

Panhard-Levassor, 1895;
Mercedes, 1904;
Duesenberg, 1921;
Maserati, 1957;
Lotus-Ford, 1963;
McLaren M16, 1971.

No one model is more difficult to make than any other. So it does not matter which you decide to make first, since you are going to make them all anyway—at least that is the author's hope. If you are a true model-maker, your enthusiasm for making these paper racing cars will increase as you go along.

The following are general instructions that will help make your model-building more successful.

1. Read the book through before starting to build any of the models. When you have decided which one to build first, read the directions for it carefully to be sure you understand all the steps. Do the same for each model you build. Before you begin, gather your materials and tools, and select construction paper in the color you want for your racing-car model.

2. To make the parts for the models, use the measurements given on the diagrams in the book. Transfer these to the construction paper or cardboard. Then draw and cut out the parts. Work with extreme care. The accuracy of your parts will determine to a great extent how well your finished model looks.

Note that some diagrams in the book are not drawn to scale. Use the *measurements* given on the diagrams to draw the parts for your model.

3. All of the racing-car models require rigid cardboard. It is used mainly for the chassis, bulkheads, and wheels. The cardboard must be rigid enough to hold its shape. As mentioned in the chapter on materials and tools, cigar boxes and matting board are excellent for this purpose. Cutting these stiff materials will require more pressure on your knife than cutting thinner paper. Draw the knife several times over the line, going deeper with each cut. Then bend the cardboard along the cut line. Turn the cardboard upright and slice through the portion, still holding the sections together. Or you may prefer to leave the cardboard flat on the work surface while repeatedly running your knife along the cut line until the pieces separate. In this case, make sure your work surface is well protected.

All the models are built on a chassis of rigid cardboard. If your cardboard does not have too much printing or design on it, leave it as is. If there is too much printing, paint it out with poster paint. You need to paint only the underside of the chassis; the top side will be hidden by the body of the car.

To make cardboard wheels, use your compass to draw a circle with the diameter called for in the diagram. Then cut it out with your scissors. To make a wheel as perfectly round as possible, go over the circle several times with your compass pencil, pressing firmly. This will make a deeply indented circle and form a track for your scissors to follow. As you cut the circle, keep turning the pattern continuously into the scissors. This will lessen the chances of cutting straight sections instead of curves around the rim of the wheel.

Draw the wheel designs before cutting out the circles. Hold the cardboard down on the work surface with small pieces of masking tape while you draw. Be careful to keep the tape clear of the wheel pattern.

4. Every model has one or more curved parts. A few parts bend more than once, forming compound curves. Here are two ideas that will help you form both simple and compound curves:

• Before gluing the part, slide it over the edge of your work table. Pull the part down gently but firmly with one hand as you press the paper against the table edge with the other hand. You can also slide the paper over the edge of your ruler in the same way. This will give the part a definite curve. Once the paper is curved in this manner, it is a lot easier to glue in position.

• For parts with compound curves—curving in one direction, then another—moisten the paper with water. Use a damp cloth or sponge; do not soak the paper. Too much water will make it tear easily. While the paper is moist, you will be able to mold it into any desired shape, however complicated. You may glue the moistened part immediately; it does not have to dry first.

5. Various lengths of drinking straws are used on several of the models for exhaust pipes and other parts. When cutting the lengths you need, insert a pencil or other round piece of wood inside the straw. This will support the section you are cutting as you run your knife around it. If you don't support it, you will crush the straw and make it unusable.

6. All the models have numbers or designs on their hoods, sides, tail ends, or wheels. These are to be drawn on the parts before gluing. Use black India ink or black crayon. If you prefer, you can cut the numbers from any color construction paper and glue them onto the model.

7. Different lengths of matchstick wood are needed for steering columns, axles, and other small parts. Note the length given in the diagram, measure this length on the matchstick with your ruler, and mark with a pencil. If you are strong enough, you can cut the wood simply by pressing down hard with your knife. Make sure the matchstick is resting on a block of scrap wood when you do this.

If the matchstick wood proves too tough for this method, place the cutting edge of the knife on the pencil mark and tap the back of the knife gently but firmly with a hammer.

There may be moments as you build the models when things seem to be going all wrong. You may start to feel that instead of cutting a part too small or gluing it on crooked, you could be having fun doing something else! But don't give up. Making car models can give you a lot of satisfaction, especially when you succeed in solving difficult shaping or gluing problems. You can't help but have a great feeling of accomplishment as you view your accurate and colorful finished models.

A final word: remember that all the suggestions above, along with others in the pages ahead, are just that—suggestions. All model-makers develop their own ways of doing things. You can draw, cut, and glue by whatever method you find easiest and most comfortable. Above all, do not hesitate to experiment. Make whatever variations you think will turn your racing car into a better-looking finished model. Good luck! And may you be first around the track!

Panhard-Levassor: 1895

This is the Panhard-Levassor that finished first in the Paris–Bordeaux–Paris race of 1895. The solid rubber tires, chain drive, and steering tiller were common features on early automobiles. Two additional headlamps were attached to the brackets at the chassis's front edge for the race.
CITROËN

René Panhard and Emile Levassor were close friends with a common interest in mechanical devices. When the automobile appeared in Europe and America in the late nineteenth century, the two Frenchmen were among the first of its enthusiastic supporters. Indeed, they were so captivated by the vehicle that they pooled their mechanical talents to build some of the first automobiles that rolled through the streets of Paris.

21

In June 1895, a Paris newspaper announced plans for a motor car race from Paris to Bordeaux and back to Paris. Panhard and Levassor immediately decided to enter the competition with one of their latest automobiles, a two-seat model. The prizes of 20,000 francs for a two-seat entry and 40,000 francs for a four-seat vehicle were certainly worth striving for. Besides, the two engineers felt that if they won, the publicity would be excellent for their business of making and selling automobiles. If they lost—well, the experience would be helpful in building improved motor cars.

The cross-country race was to be no easy drive. It was a grueling competition for vehicles still in the primitive stages of development. The round-trip journey was about 739 miles long over stony dirt roads, far less comfortable than modern concrete highways.

The two-seat car Panhard and Levassor chose for the race was powered by a gasoline (or petrol) engine. Fifteen other entries were also propelled by internal-combustion engines. Six others were steam-powered, and one had an electric motor. The engine of the Panhard-Levassor was a two-cylinder unit perfected a short time earlier by Gottlieb Daimler of Germany. He too became a famous pioneer in the early development of the automobile. Although it produced a limited amount of power, the small Daimler engine was the most efficient and dependable gasoline engine of its day; it propelled the Panhard-Levassor at an average speed of almost 15 miles per hour, a respectable rate in 1895.

The Daimler engine had to be started by several turns of a hand crank extending from the front end of the vehicle. It was not until the late 1920s that the self-starter became a standard feature on automobiles.

The race began on June 11 under a sunny Paris sky. One by one the contestants crossed the starting line to the cheers and waves of hundreds of spectators. Soon the drivers were out of the city and rolling along country roads. Several cars quickly developed problems and fell by the wayside. But Levassor, driving alone in his own car, kept moving smoothly in the little two-seater. Not very long after leaving Paris, he was far in the lead of a long line of stragglers.

As night fell, Levassor stopped briefly to light his oil-burning carriage lamps. Although their light was weak and flickering, they were better than no light at all for the narrow, rough road over which he was traveling. Levassor pushed on again through the darkness at a reduced speed.

His dependable Daimler engine and sturdy car brought Levassor to Bordeaux in twenty-four hours, far ahead of his nearest competitor. A racing official checked him in; then, after a two-hour rest, Levassor hopped into the car and headed back for Paris. He seemed determined to show that his stamina equaled that of his rugged little automobile.

On the way back, Levassor met the first of the other drivers slowly chugging southward to Bordeaux. He was confident now of winning in his division, provided nothing happened to his car. And nothing did happen, aside from a minor collision with a road obstruction. Levassor rolled into Paris an easy winner in the two-seater class. He had covered the round-trip distance of nearly 740 miles in 48 hours and 42 minutes. The victory was a remarkable demonstration of how far the automobile had advanced for its time.

The model you will build is the two-seater Panhard-Levassor, winner of the Paris–Bordeaux–Paris cross-country race in 1895.

BUILDING THE PANHARD-LEVASSOR MODEL

Chassis (Diagram 1)

Draw and cut the chassis as shown in diagram 1. Use rigid cardboard.

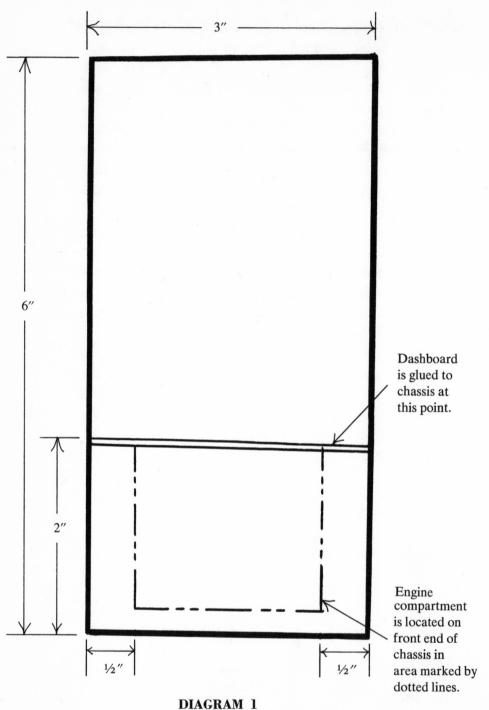

3″

6″

2″

½″

½″

Dashboard
is glued to
chassis at
this point.

Engine
compartment
is located on
front end of
chassis in
area marked by
dotted lines.

DIAGRAM 1
Chassis

Make 1 from rigid cardboard.

Engine Compartment (Diagrams 2-3)

Make the engine compartment from construction paper, using any color you wish. This will become the main color of your model. Draw and cut the compartment as shown in diagram 2.

Draw the designs and number on the appropriate panels (see diagram 2). Use a pen and black India ink for this, or black crayon. Then fold the compartment, glue it together, and glue it to the chassis.

The top of the engine compartment is a separate piece. Draw and cut the top as shown in diagram 3. Be extra careful to fold the dotted lines straight. This will help make the top piece fit better. Make sure the top fits properly, and then glue it to the engine compartment. There is no bottom piece for the compartment, since the chassis will cover this opening.

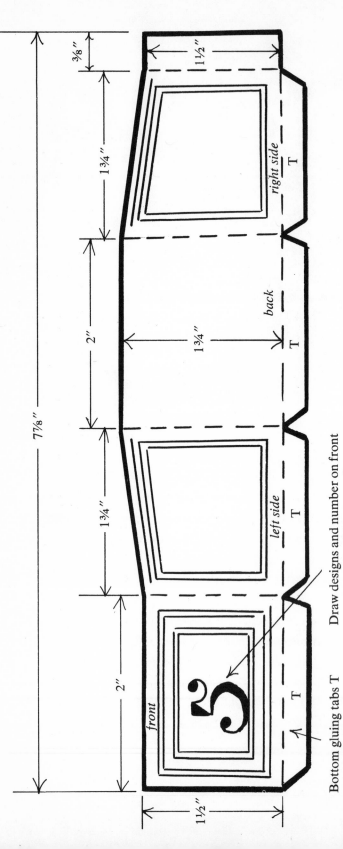

3/8"

1 1/2"

1 3/4"

right side   T

2"

1 3/4"

back   T

left side   T   T

2"

front   T   T

1 3/4"

1 1/2"

7 7/8"

Bottom gluing tabs T
are 1/4" wide.
Fold tabs inward
to glue engine
compartment to chassis.

Draw designs and number on front
and sides before folding.

DIAGRAM 2
Engine Compartment

Make 1 from construction paper.

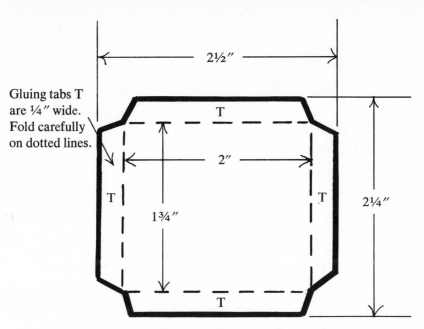

Gluing tabs **T** are ¼″ wide. Fold carefully on dotted lines.

2½″

2″

1¾″

2¼″

T
T
T
T

Engine Compartment Top

Make 1 from construction paper.

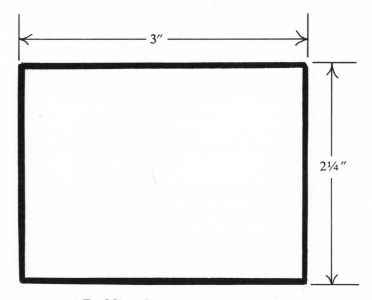

3″

2¼″

Dashboard

Make 1 from rigid cardboard.

DIAGRAM 3

Dashboard (Diagram 3)

The dashboard of the Panhard-Levassor model is made of rigid cardboard. The same material used for the chassis would be good. Draw and cut the dashboard as shown in diagram 3. You may either paint the dashboard with poster paint or cover it with construction paper. Whichever method you use, the color should be different from that of the engine compartment. When finished, the dashboard is glued against the rear side of the engine compartment.

Floor Mat (Diagram 4)

The floor mat covers the chassis between the dashboard and the driver's seat. Use any color construction paper you wish. Draw and cut the mat as shown in diagram 4. Glue the mat to the chassis, putting one edge tight against the bottom edge of the dashboard. Rub your finger over the surface of the mat for a minute or two to make sure the piece is firmly glued.

Passenger Compartment (Diagrams 4-5)

The most difficult part of the Panhard-Levassor model to construct is the passenger compartment. It is made in three main sections—two side panels and a rear panel. Make all three panels of the same color construction paper as the engine compartment. Draw and cut the panels as shown in diagrams 4 and 5. Make them as carefully as you can, since their neatness will add to the attractiveness of your finished model.

Before assembling the compartment, draw the line designs on all the panels and the number on the back panel as shown in the diagrams.

Side and Rear Cushions (Diagrams 5-6)

The cushions may be made of any color construction paper you wish. Draw the designs on them with pen and black India ink. See diagrams 5 and 6 for the shape of the cushions and the designs to be drawn.

DIAGRAM 4

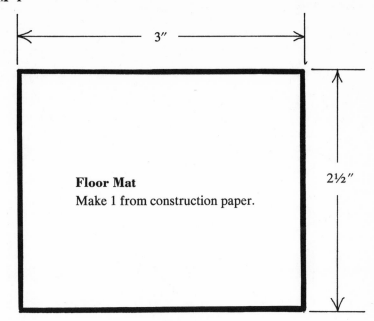

3″

2½″

Floor Mat
Make 1 from construction paper.

Draw these lines with black ink. Be sure to draw on opposite sides of the two pieces so you will have a left and a right side panel.

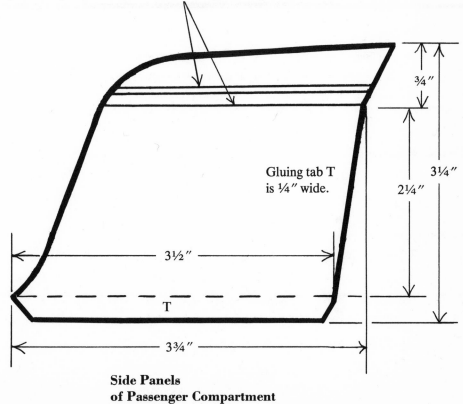

¾″

3¼″

2¼″

Gluing tab T
is ¼″ wide.

3½″

T

3¾″

**Side Panels
of Passenger Compartment**

Make 2 from construction paper.

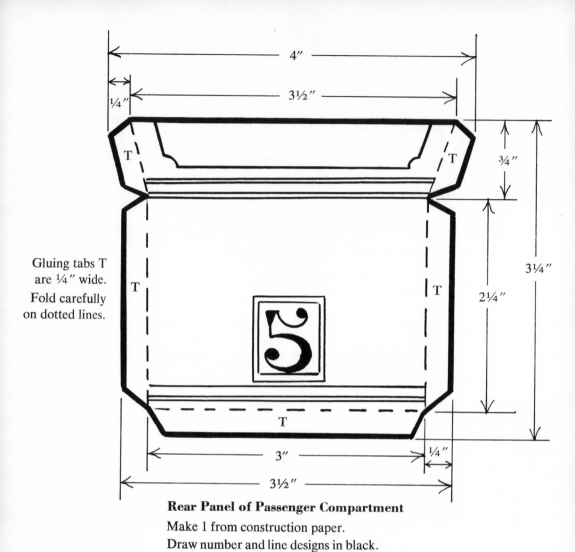

4″

3½″

¼″

T   T

¾″

Gluing tabs T
are ¼″ wide.
Fold carefully
on dotted lines.

T   5   T

3¼″

2¼″

T

3″   ¼″

3½″

Rear Panel of Passenger Compartment
Make 1 from construction paper.
Draw number and line designs in black.

DIAGRAM 5

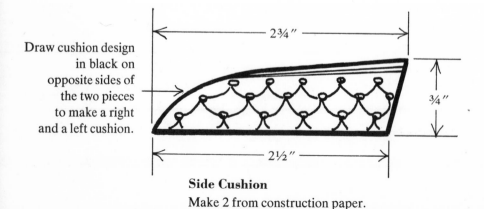

2¾″

Draw cushion design
in black on
opposite sides of
the two pieces
to make a right
and a left cushion.

¾″

2½″

Side Cushion
Make 2 from construction paper.

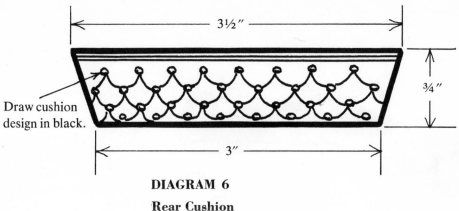

Draw cushion design in black.

3½″

¾″

3″

DIAGRAM 6

Rear Cushion
Make 1 from construction paper.

Glue the finished cushions on the inside of the side and rear panels of the passenger compartment. The photo of the finished model shows how the cushions look when in place.

After you have finished making the panels with their cushions, glue them to the chassis *one at a time*. Make sure that the rear panel is glued even with the back edge of the chassis and the two side panels are glued even with the side edges of the chassis. Finally, join the two side panels to the rear panel, making sure that the two rear corners meet squarely. See the photos of the finished model, pages 25, 44, and 52.

Seat (Diagram 7)

The seat is made of the same color construction paper as the side and rear cushions. Draw and cut the seat as shown in diagram 7. Draw the cushion design, the same as that of the side and rear cushions, before assembling and gluing the seat. Use pen and black India ink for this.

Try fitting the seat in place before gluing. It may be necessary to trim it here and there to make it fit properly. See the photo of the finished model to check its position. Once you are satisfied, glue it in place.

31

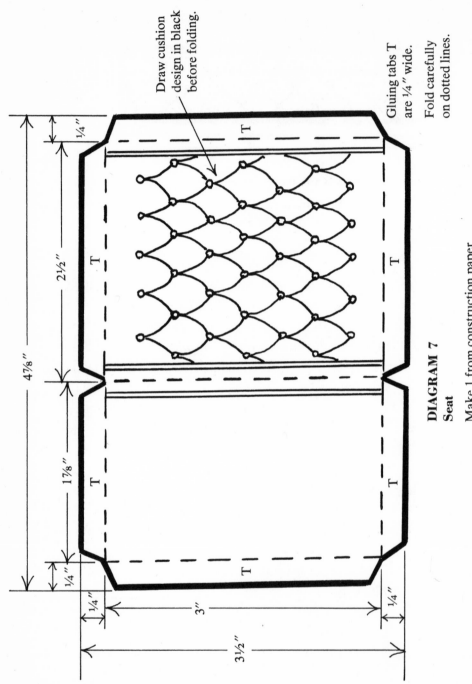

Draw cushion design in black before folding.

Gluing tabs T are ¼″ wide.

Fold carefully on dotted lines.

¼″

2½″

4⅞″

1⅞″

¼″

¼″

3″

3½″

¼″

DIAGRAM 7
Seat

Make 1 from construction paper.

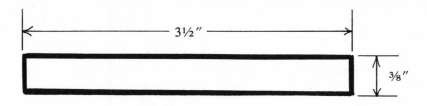

DIAGRAM 8
Axle Support
Make 2 from rigid cardboard.

Axle Supports (Diagram 8)

Two axle supports for the wheels are needed. These are made of
rigid cardboard. Draw and cut them as shown in diagram 8.
Paint the supports yellow or any other color, using poster paint.

Each support is glued on its narrow edge, perpendicular to
the underside of the chassis. The front axle support is attached
¾ inch in from the front end of the chassis. The rear axle support is glued 1 inch in from the back end of the chassis. It will
help to measure these distances and mark the locations with a
pencil line before gluing. The axle supports extend beyond the
chassis at both side edges.

Front Apron (Diagram 9)

The Panhard-Levassor had front and rear aprons hanging down
from the chassis. On the model both these parts are made from
construction paper; use the same color paper as the dashboard.
Draw and cut the front apron as shown in diagram 9. Lay the
apron flat on your work table and draw the line and circle design on one side as shown. Use pen and India ink or black
crayon. Also, before attaching the front apron, be sure to make
the small hole as shown in the diagram. This will be needed for
gluing the crank handle to the apron.

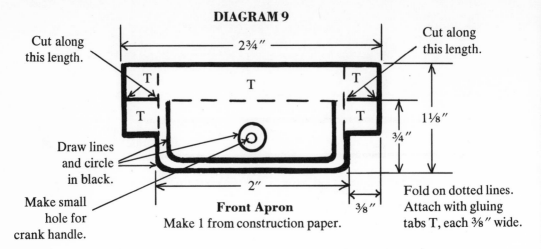

DIAGRAM 9

Cut along this length.

Cut along this length.

2¾″

T   T

T   T

T   T

1⅛″

¾″

Draw lines and circle in black.

2″

⅜″

Make small hole for crank handle.

Front Apron

Make 1 from construction paper.

Fold on dotted lines. Attach with gluing tabs T, each ⅜″ wide.

When finished, glue the front apron to the underside of the chassis at the very front edge. Be sure the design side faces forward. See the photo of the finished model on page 52.

Rear Apron (Diagram 10)

The rear apron is a simpler piece. Make it from the same color construction paper as the front apron. Draw and cut the rear apron as shown in diagram 10. Fold it and attach it with the 3-inch gluing tab to the underside of the chassis at the very rear edge.

Front Springs (Diagram 10)

The Panhard-Levassor model has four springs—two in the front and two in the rear. They are made of rigid cardboard and drawn upon to represent leaf springs. Before the development of coil springs, leaf springs were the only kind used on early cars.

Draw and cut four front spring pieces; you will use one piece for the top and one piece for the bottom of each spring. Draw the design on one side of each piece. Also cut four short ¼-inch pins from round toothpicks; paint these black with India ink or poster paint. Glue two of these pins across the ends of one spring piece, making sure you glue them on the side without the design (see diagram 10). Then glue the other half of the spring to the pins to form a kind of sandwich. Again, be sure the de-

34

DIAGRAM 10

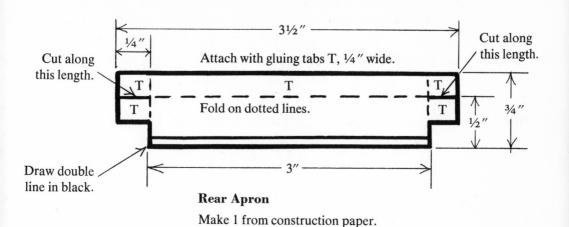

Rear Apron

Make 1 from construction paper.

Draw design
in black
on one side
of each piece.

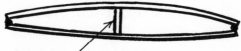

Front Spring
Make 4 from rigid cardboard.

¼″

Pin
Make 4 from round
toothpicks.

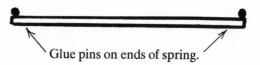

Glue pins on ends of spring.

Spring is glued to end of
front axle support.

Front spring to look as above
when attached to model.

sign is on the outside. When the spring is assembled, you should see the design on the top and bottom sides.

After the top and bottom parts of each spring are firmly glued, slide one completed spring over each end of the front axle support that extends beyond the left and right edges of the chassis. The support will spread apart the top and bottom sections of the spring into a bow-like shape.

Glue the springs at the points where they touch the edges of the axle supports. Also glue the springs where they meet the edges of the chassis. This will attach the springs more firmly in their horizontal position.

Rear Springs (Diagram 11)

The two rear springs are made the same way as the front springs. The only difference is that the rear springs are longer. You will have to draw and cut the same number of parts—four spring sections and four ¼-inch pins. The design of the spring leaves is also drawn the same way. The rear springs are attached in the same manner as the front pair: slide them over the extended ends of the rear axle support, turn them parallel to the chassis, and glue.

Rear Fenders (Diagram 12)

The two rear fenders are made of black construction paper. Draw and cut the fenders as shown in diagram 12.

Attach the fenders to the right and left side panels of the passenger compartment. They should curve toward the front and extend straight toward the rear. Be sure to keep the straight top portion of the fender on or slightly below the parallel lines drawn on the side panels. See diagram 13 for placing and gluing the fenders. The lower curved portion of each fender can be held in position by gluing it to the front end of the rear spring.

DIAGRAM 11
Rear Spring

Make 4 from rigid cardboard.

Draw design in black on one side of each piece.

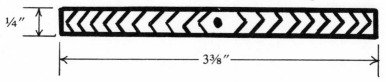

¼″

3⅜″

¼″

Pin
Make 4 from round
toothpicks.

Glue pins on ends of spring.

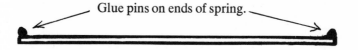

Rear spring to look as above
when attached to model.
Spring is glued to end of
rear axle support.

DIAGRAM 12

Fold gluing tabs T on dotted lines.

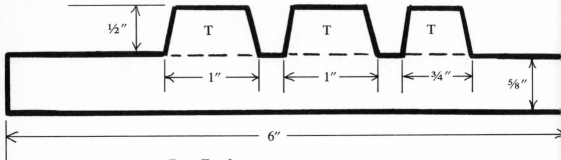

Rear Fender
Make 2 from black construction paper.

Bend at sharp right angle on dotted line.

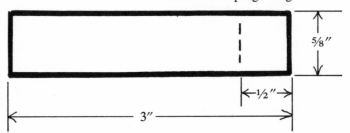

Front Fender
Make 2 from black construction paper.

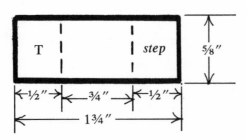

Step
Make 2 from black construction paper.
Fold on dotted lines into "Z" shape.

DIAGRAM 13

Attaching Fenders and Steps

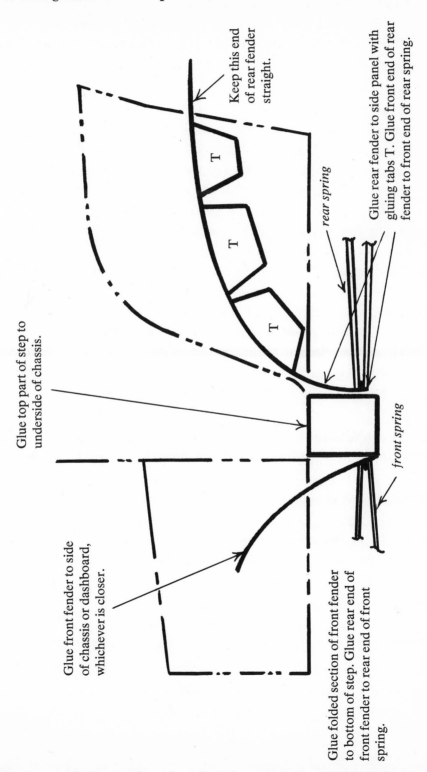

Keep this end of rear fender straight.

Glue rear fender to side panel with gluing tabs T. Glue front end of rear fender to front end of rear spring.

rear spring

Glue top part of step to underside of chassis.

front spring

Glue front fender to side of chassis or dashboard, whichever is closer.

Glue folded section of front fender to bottom of step. Glue rear end of front fender to rear end of front spring.

T T T

Front Fenders (Diagram 12)

The two front fenders of the Panhard-Levassor model are also made from black construction paper. Draw and cut them as shown in diagram 12. They are attached along with the steps.

Steps (Diagram 12)

Draw and cut the two steps from black construction paper (see diagram 12). One step is glued on the right side of the passenger compartment and one on the left. When attached, each step should have a "Z" shape, except that the middle bar is straight up and down rather than at a slant (⌐⌐).

The top part of the step (gluing tab T) is glued to the underside of the chassis, almost in line with the dashboard above it. See diagram 13 for proper placement. The bottom part of the "Z" step is glued on top of the short piece of the front fender that extends rearward. This also attaches the front fender to the car. To make the front fenders more secure, put a little glue at the point where they touch the edges of the dashboard or chassis. Also glue the fenders at the point where they touch the back ends of the front springs (see diagram 13).

Front Wheels (Diagram 14)

The two front wheels of the Panhard-Levassor model are drawn and cut from rigid cardboard as shown in diagram 14. The cardboard should be white so the wheel design can be clearly seen. Draw the design on both sides of each wheel with pen and India ink. Remember, when cutting the circles for the wheels, keep pushing the cardboard continuously into the scissors.

Rear Wheels (Diagram 14)

The two rear wheels are larger than the front pair. They are cut from the same rigid cardboard, and the same wheel design is drawn on both sides of each wheel. Diagram 14 shows the size and design for the rear wheels.

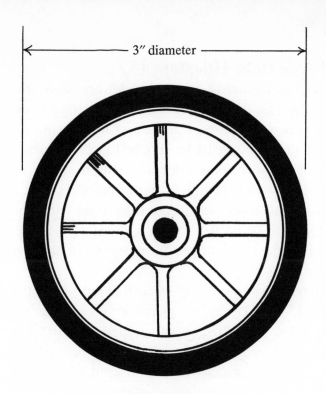

3″ diameter

Front Wheel

Make 2 from
rigid cardboard.

Draw tire,
spokes, and
hubcap in black.

DIAGRAM 14

Rear Wheel

Make 2 from
rigid cardboard.

Draw tire,
spokes, and
hubcap in black.

3½″ diameter

Axles and Axle Hubs (Diagram 15)

The axles for the Panhard-Levassor model are made of large wooden matchsticks. You will make four short axles, rather than the usual two long ones. Each wheel has a separate axle assembly so it can more easily be attached to the model.

Cut each of the four short axles to a length of 1¾ inches. Paint them black with India ink or poster paint. For each axle hub, cut four small triangular pieces from rigid cardboard (a total of sixteen will be needed for all four axles). See diagram 15 for the size and shape of the triangles. Paint these pieces black like the axles.

Glue four triangles to one end of each axle to form the hub (see diagram 15). Make sure the pieces are glued exactly at the ends of the axles. These pieces are needed for attaching the wheels; if they are crooked, your wheels will be crooked too. When glued, the four pieces will form a kind of cross pattern with two pieces at right angles to the other two pieces.

After you have finished assembling the axles, glue them to the wheels. You can do this best by placing a wheel flat on your working surface. Put lots of glue on the edges of the axle hub and press this onto the center of the wheel. Make certain that the axle is in the center of the wheel and in a straight up and down position, as in diagram 15. You will have to judge this by eye as best you can.

Attaching the Wheels to the Model

When all four wheels have been glued to their individual axles, attach them to the model. Place a generous amount of glue on one side of the axle extending from a front wheel. Slide the axle through the spring and against the forward side of the front axle support. Hold the wheel and axle assembly for a few moments until the glue hardens and there is no danger of the unit falling off. Be patient; the wheels are heavy and you have to be absolutely certain the glue is holding them in position.

DIAGRAM 15

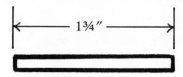

Axle
Make 4 from
large matchsticks.

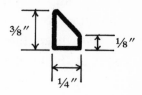

Axle Hub
Make 16 from
rigid cardboard.

Axle Hub Assembly
Glue 4 hub pieces to one end of each axle.

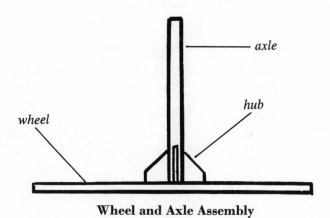

Wheel and Axle Assembly

Follow the same procedure for the remaining wheels. Remember that the axles of the front wheels are glued to the front side of the front axle support, and the axles of the rear wheels to the rear side of the rear axle support. Also make sure while mounting the wheels that they are equally spaced, ⅜ inch from the edges of the chassis.

Steering Lever (Diagram 16)

The Panhard-Levassor's driver sat on the right side of the car, and steered by means of a steering lever rather than a wheel. Later, on more advanced cars, steering wheels took the place of levers.

On this model, the steering lever consists of three wooden parts. Two of these parts are made from lengths of large wooden matchsticks, and one part from a length of a round toothpick. See diagram 16 for the proper lengths to cut.

DIAGRAM 16
Steering Lever

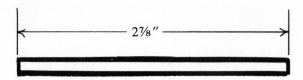

← —————————— 2⅞″ —————————— →

Part #1
Make 1 from large matchstick.
Paint black.

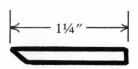

← — 1¼″ — →

½″

Part #2
Make 1 from large matchstick.
Paint yellow.

Part #3
Make 1 from
round toothpick.
Paint black.

Steering Lever Assembly   part #2   ← — part #3

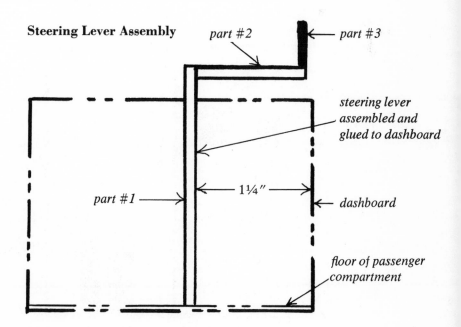

steering lever
assembled and
glued to dashboard

part #1 ——→   ← — 1¼″ — →   ← — dashboard

floor of passenger
compartment

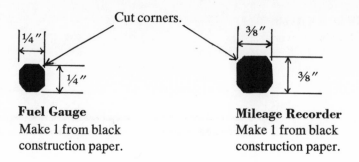

Fuel Gauge
Make 1 from black
construction paper.

Mileage Recorder
Make 1 from black
construction paper.

DIAGRAM 17

Foot Brake Pedal
Make 1 from
rigid cardboard.
Paint black.

Gas Pedal
Make 1 from
rigid cardboard.
Paint black.

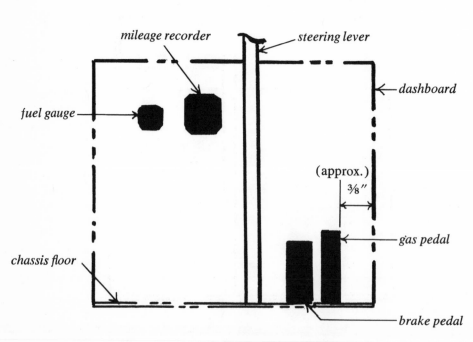

Location of Gauges and Foot Pedals

The longer piece of matchstick, glued to the dashboard, is painted black. Use India ink or poster paint. The short piece of matchstick is painted yellow, or any other color, with poster paint. The third and shortest piece of the lever, made from a toothpick, is painted black.

Assemble all three pieces of the steering lever as shown in diagram 16. When they are all firmly attached, glue the lever to the inside of the dashboard; diagram 16 shows the lever's correct placement. While gluing the steering lever, keep it upright as much as possible.

Gauges (Diagram 17)

A fuel gauge and a mileage recorder are the two instruments needed on the Panhard-Levassor model. Both are made from black construction paper. See diagram 17 for the shapes to be drawn and cut. Also, the diagram will help you to place and glue them correctly on the dashboard.

Gas Pedal and Foot Brake Pedal (Diagram 17)

The gas pedal and the foot brake pedal are both made from rigid cardboard. See diagram 17 for the shapes to be drawn and cut. They are glued to the lower right-hand corner of the dashboard at an angle. The upper ends are attached to the dashboard and the lower ends to the floor of the passenger compartment. See diagram 17 for the correct locations.

Hand Shift, Hand Brake, Handgrip, and Holder (Diagram 18)

The hand shift and hand brake are made from lengths of round toothpicks. They are both the same; see diagram 18 for the lengths to cut and method of construction. The short, ⅜-inch long handgrips are glued to one end of both the shift and the brake, as the diagram indicates. The grips and upper portions of both the brake and the shift are painted yellow with poster

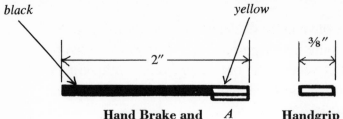

Hand Brake and Hand Shift
Make 2 from round toothpicks.

A

Handgrip A
Make 2 from round toothpicks. Paint yellow. Glue one handgrip to top of hand shift and hand brake.

DIAGRAM 18

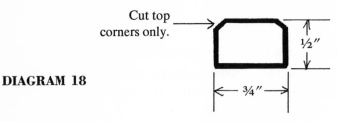

Cut top corners only.

½"

¾"

Holder
Make 1 from rigid cardboard. Paint yellow.

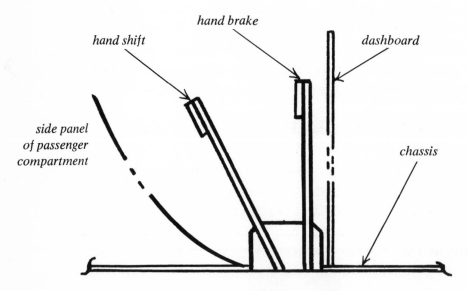

Hand Shift, Hand Brake, and Holder Assembly

paint. The remaining parts of both the shift and the brake are painted black with India ink or poster paint. Diagram 18 shows these painted sections.

Both the shift and the brake are glued to a holder. Make it from a piece of rigid cardboard and paint it with yellow poster paint. See diagram 18 for the shape to be drawn and cut. Attach the shift and brake to the holder as in diagram 18.

When this shift-brake assembly is finished, glue it to the side of the model; place it at the edge of the chassis on the right, close to the dashboard. See diagram 18 and the photo of the finished model on page 25.

Carriage Lamps (Diagrams 19-20)

The Panhard-Levassor model has two large carriage lamps mounted on the top corners of the dashboard. They are made of yellow, green, and black construction paper and round wooden toothpicks.

The body of each lamp is made from a strip of yellow construction paper 2½ inches long and ½ inch wide. Roll the strip around a thick pencil or rod or even over the edge of your work table. This will curl the paper and make it easier to shape into the cylinder or ring. Bring the two loose ends together and overlap them until the diameter of the ring measures about ¾ inch. Use your ruler to make this measurement. Then glue the overlapping ends. Hold the ends together for a few moments until the glue hardens.

After the two rings are made as much the same size as possible, cut two rear discs, also from yellow construction paper. These must have the same ¾-inch diameter as the rings. Press hard on your compass while drawing the circles. This will make a deep impression in the paper and help you cut a more perfect circle. Glue a disc to one open end of each ring. Put glue on the rim of the ring and press the disc to it. Place a small weight, such as a coin, on the disc as the ring rests on your work table to help make the attachment more secure.

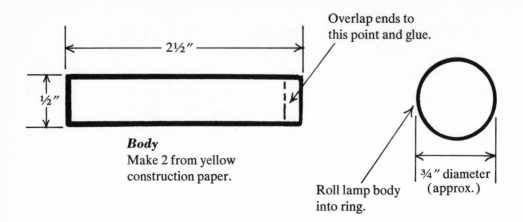

Body
Make 2 from yellow
construction paper.

2½"

½"

Overlap ends to
this point and glue.

Roll lamp body
into ring.

¾" diameter
(approx.)

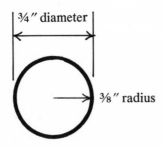

¾" diameter

⅜" radius

Rear Disc
Make 2 from yellow
construction paper.

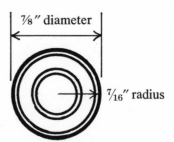

⅞" diameter

⁷⁄₁₆" radius

Front Disc
Make 2 from green
construction paper.

Draw circles in black.

**DIAGRAM 19
Carriage Lamp**

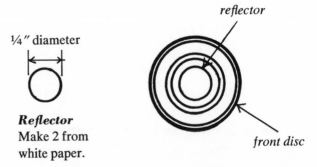

¼" diameter

Reflector
Make 2 from
white paper.

reflector

front disc

Glue reflectors in center of front discs.

DIAGRAM 20
Carriage Lamp

1/4"

Top Post
Make 2 from
round toothpicks.
Paint black.

5/16" diameter

Cap for Top Post
Make 2 from black
construction paper.

5/8"

Bottom Post
Make 2 from
round toothpicks.
Paint black.

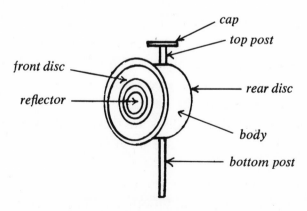

cap

top post

front disc

rear disc

reflector

body

bottom post

Carriage Lamp Assembly

While the rear discs are becoming firmly glued, cut a pair of front discs from light-green construction paper. These discs are ⅞ inch in diameter. On one side of each front disc, draw a series of circles with your compass and then go over them with black ink (see diagram 19). These circles, one set inside the other, represent the rims of the frame and the glass.

Next draw and cut two reflector discs from white paper, ¼ inch in diameter (see diagram 19). Glue one reflector disc onto the center of each large green front disc, inside the circles you drew. This will give the carriage lamps a more realistic look.

The completed front discs are then glued to the open or front end of each lamp ring. See diagram 20 and the photo of the finished model.

For the top lamp posts, cut two ¼-inch pieces from the thick center portion of a round toothpick. Then cut two small discs, ⁵⁄₁₆ inch in diameter, from black construction paper. These are the caps for the top posts. Glue a cap to one end of each ¼-inch piece, forming two toadstool-shaped units. Paint both units black with India ink or poster paint. When completed, the two units are glued to the top center of each lamp. See diagram 20 and the photo of the finished model.

Again using the thick portion of round toothpicks, cut two pieces ⅝ inch long for the bottom posts (see diagram 20). Paint both lengths black. Glue one piece to the bottom of each lamp; try to place them directly under the toadstool-shaped units on top of the lamps. Once these bottom posts are firmly attached, your carriage lamps will be completed. Glue them to the outside top corners of the dashboard, as in the photo of the finished model.

Head Lamps (Diagram 21)

In addition to the two carriage lamps, the Panhard-Levassor model has two small head lamps. These are made the same way as the carriage lamps; however, they are smaller in diameter and they do not have any wood attachments.

The body of each lamp is made from a strip of light-green construction paper ½ inch wide and 2 inches long. Form and glue each strip into a ring with a diameter of about ½ inch. Draw and cut two rear discs, ½ inch in diameter, from the same light-green construction paper. Glue one of these discs to an open end of each ring.

Draw and cut two larger front discs, ⅝ inch in diameter, from yellow construction paper. On one side of each front disc, draw a series of circles with your compass (see diagram 21) and go over them with black ink. Then glue one front disc to the open end of each ring. Be sure the side with the circles faces out. Diagram 21 shows how the head lamps look when assembled.

The head lamps are glued to the front edge of the chassis on each side of the engine compartment. See the photo of the finished model.

53

Overlap ends to this point and glue.

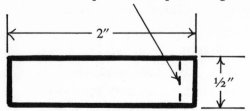

Body
Make 2 from green
construction paper.

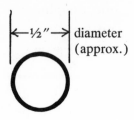

diameter
(approx.)

Roll lamp body into ring.

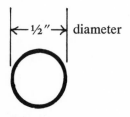

diameter

Rear Disc
Make 2 from green
construction paper.

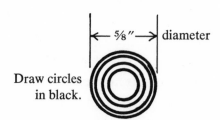

Draw circles
in black.

Front Disc
Make 2 from yellow
construction paper.

front disc

body

rear disc

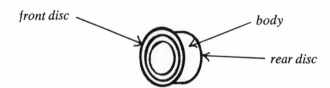

Head Lamp Assembly

DIAGRAM 21
Head Lamp

Taillight (Diagram 22)

The Panhard-Levassor has one taillight. It is made much like the head lamps.

The body of the taillight is rolled from a strip of light-green construction paper as shown in diagram 22. Roll the paper strip around a thick pencil and glue the ends together to form a ring about ½ inch in diameter.

Next draw and cut two discs, also ½ inch in diameter, from orange construction paper. Glue these discs to the open ends of the ring. After assembling the taillight, glue it to the lower left corner of the rear of the body.

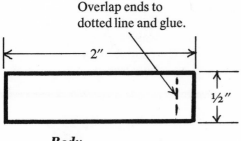

Body
Make 1 from green
construction paper.

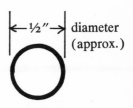

Roll taillight
body into ring.

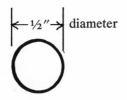

Disc
Make 2 from orange
construction paper.

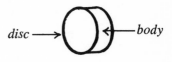

Taillight Assembly

DIAGRAM 22
Taillight

Crank Handle (Diagram 23)

The Panhard-Levassor's crank handle is made from lengths of round toothpicks; see diagram 23 for the lengths to cut and the colors to be used. The diagram also shows how to assemble the crank handle. The finished piece will have a "Z" shape, except that the vertical part is straight rather than slanted.

Glue the crank handle to the front end of the model, inserting it in the hole in the front apron. Position the crank handle at an angle rather than straight up and down.

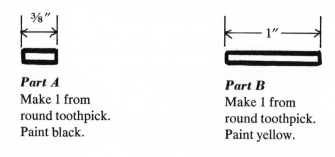

Part A
Make 1 from
round toothpick.
Paint black.

Part B
Make 1 from
round toothpick.
Paint yellow.

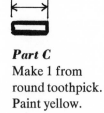

Part C
Make 1 from
round toothpick.
Paint yellow.

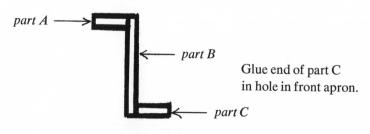

Glue end of part C
in hole in front apron.

Crank Handle Assembly

DIAGRAM 23
Crank Handle

Passenger Compartment Hood (Diagram 24)

The hood is made in three separate sections—two for the tops of the side panels and one for the top of the rear panel. The hood sections are drawn and cut from black construction paper (see diagram 24). Each section is folded in accordion pleats along the dotted lines. When finished, the sections are glued along the top edges of the side and rear panels. See the photos of the finished model, pages 25, 44, and 52.

This completes your model of the 1895 Panhard-Levassor, winner of one of the earliest cross-country races.

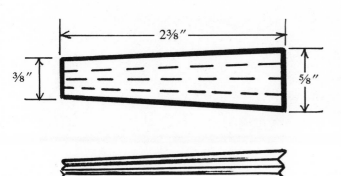

Side Section
Make 2 from
black construction paper.

Fold on dotted lines–
first one way,
then the other–
to make accordion
pleats.

Folded side section should look as above.

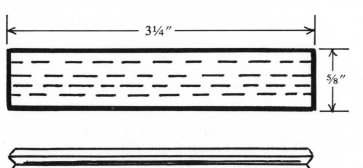

Rear Section
Make 1 from black
construction paper.

Fold on dotted lines–
first one way,
then the other–
to make accordion
pleats.

Folded rear section should look as above.

DIAGRAM 24
Passenger Compartment Hood

Mercedes: 1904

The powerful Mercedes racer of the early 1900s had few equals on the track or in inter-city road races. A 1904 model was driven to a world land speed record by the American sportsman William K. Vanderbilt.
MERCEDES-BENZ

Mercedes is one of the great names in automobile history. During the early 1900s, the Mercedes with its powerful engine, speed, and durability became the scourge of road racing in Europe and America. Perhaps the high point in its racing record occurred in 1914 in the Grand Prix at Lyons, France. In that historic road competition a team of Mercedes racers captured the first three places. Racing victories brought fame not only to the vehicle and drivers—Camille Jenatzy and Christian

Lautenschlager, for example—but also a healthy boost in business for the car's German manufacturer.

Ten years earlier, the Mercedes of 1904 had acquired special renown when it captured the crown as the world's fastest automobile. The driver on this record-breaking run was William K. Vanderbilt, a wealthy American sportsman.

Fascinated by the speed of automobiles, Vanderbilt had set one world speed mark in 1902 when he drove a French-built Mors at a rate of 76 miles per hour. By 1904 the record had been boosted to 91 miles per hour. This was established by Henry Ford, destined to become one of the biggest motor car manufacturers in the United States. Ford had made the record speed dash in a car of his own make over the frozen surface of a lake near Detroit, Michigan. When Vanderbilt read of his fellow American's success, he considered it a challenge and immediately made plans to regain the speed crown.

Vanderbilt decided to make his attempt with a powerful Mercedes. He had been impressed by the car's outstanding performances in road races throughout Europe. He bought a gleaming white Mercedes, the latest in the 1904 series, and had it shipped to Daytona Beach, Florida.

At the turn of the century Daytona Beach was fast becoming a favorite course for automobile speed enthusiasts. Miles of open beach with hard-packed sand made an ideal space for driving cars at top speed. By the end of January Vanderbilt was ready to make his speed run. Stopwatch timers were stationed at the beginning and end of the mile-long course. The engine of the big Mercedes was warmed up, its rumbling roar echoing over the beach. The engine had only four cylinders, but they were huge—fat as baby pickle barrels—and capable of pumping out more than 90 horsepower.

At the signal, Vanderbilt, hunched over and gripping the steering wheel tightly with both hands, came booming full tilt to the starting line. He roared over the mile stretch, then waited

anxiously for the figures to be calculated. A smile crossed his face when he heard the news—92.30 miles per hour, a new world record. Once again Vanderbilt was the auto speed king of the world.

After nearly three quarters of a century, Mercedes (now Mercedes-Benz) is still a prominent name in the auto industry. Today, however, it is no longer seen on racing cars. The name is reserved for superbly engineered pleasure cars, buses, and trucks.

The model you will build is the 1904 Mercedes in which Vanderbilt set his new speed record.

BUILDING THE MERCEDES MODEL

Chassis (Diagrams 1-2)
The chassis of the Mercedes model is made from a piece of rigid

cardboard, 8½ inches long and 2½ inches wide (see diagram 1). Two strips of rigid cardboard, 9¾ inches long and ¼ inch wide, are made for the underside of the chassis. One end of each strip is cut in a curve (see diagram 2). The strips are glued edgewise (perpendicular to the chassis) along the right and left edges of the chassis. The curved ends will extend beyond the chassis and become the front of the car. The straight ends of the strips should be even with the back end of the chassis.

After the side strips are firmly glued, paint them black with poster paint or India ink; see diagram 2 and the photo of the finished model.

Radiator and Dashboard (Diagrams 3-4)

The motor compartment of the Mercedes is made up of three sections—front (radiator), back (dashboard), and hood. Use construction paper of whatever color you wish for these parts. Make the radiator and dashboard ends first; see diagrams 3 and 4. Do not forget to include the gluing tabs, marked T. Measure your dimensions accurately and fold the dotted lines carefully; score the dotted lines with the point of a knife before folding.

Draw the radiator grill design, using India ink or black crayon, on one side of the radiator (see diagram 3). On the dashboard, make a small hole on the right side for the steering column. See diagram 4 for the exact location of the hole. Use the point of your scissors or a nail to make the hole; if necessary, enlarge it by twirling the point of a pencil in it.

Gauges (Diagram 3)

Three gauges are needed for the Mercedes model—a speedometer, a gas gauge, and an oil gauge. These are drawn and cut from black construction paper and then glued to the dashboard. See diagram 3 for their sizes and shapes.

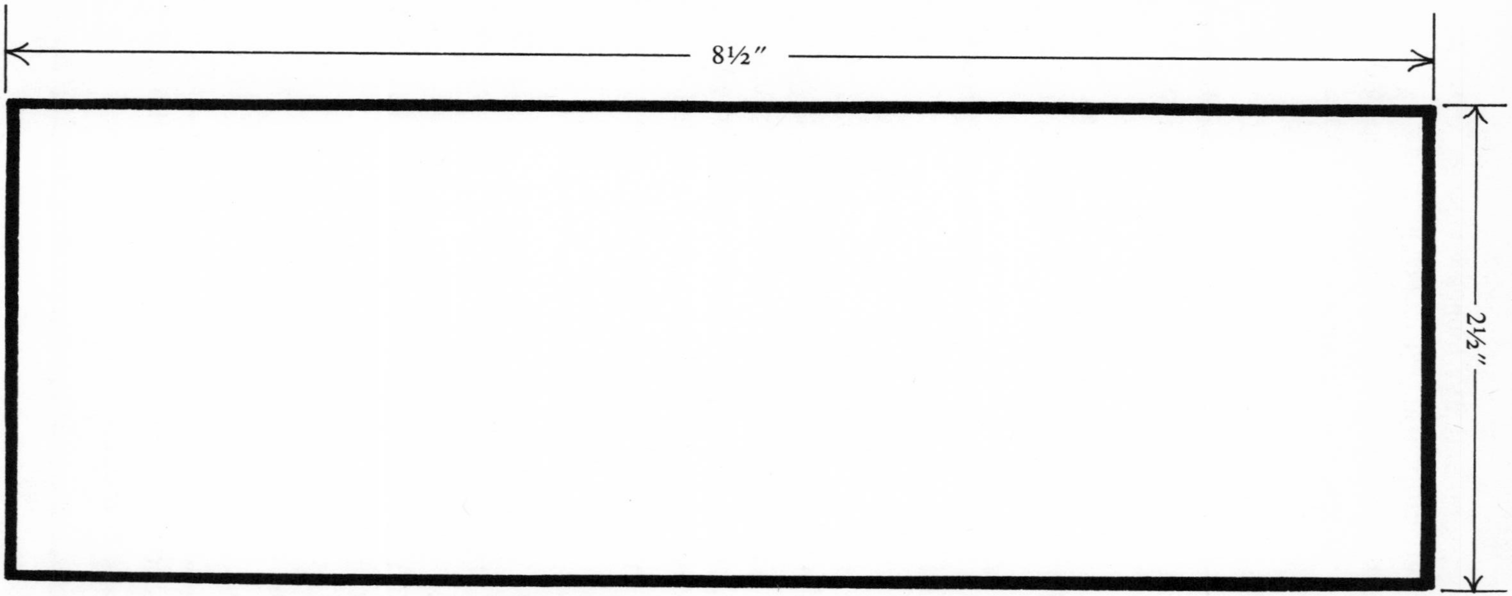

2½"

8½"

DIAGRAM 1
Chassis
Make 1 from rigid cardboard.

Note: This diagram is not to scale. Cut the chassis
to the measurements given.

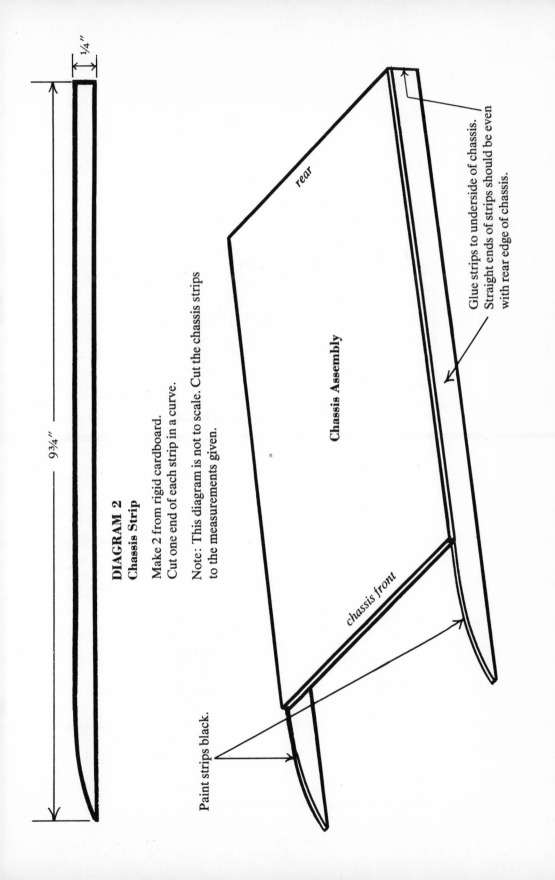

¼"

9¾"

DIAGRAM 2
Chassis Strip

Make 2 from rigid cardboard.
Cut one end of each strip in a curve.

Note: This diagram is not to scale. Cut the chassis strips
to the measurements given.

rear

Chassis Assembly

Glue strips to underside of chassis.
Straight ends of strips should be even
with rear edge of chassis.

chassis front

Paint strips black.

DIAGRAM 3

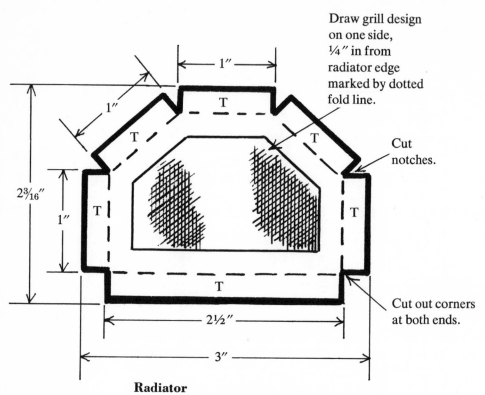

Draw grill design on one side, ¼″ in from radiator edge marked by dotted fold line.

1″

1″

1″

2³⁄₁₆″

2½″

3″

T

Cut notches.

Cut out corners at both ends.

Radiator
Make 1 from construction paper.
Gluing tabs T are ¼″ wide.

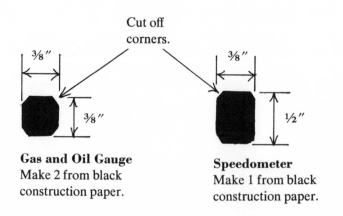

Cut off corners.

⅜″

⅜″

⅜″

½″

Gas and Oil Gauge
Make 2 from black
construction paper.

Speedometer
Make 1 from black
construction paper.

64

Glue the speedometer in place first. It should be in the top center of the dashboard. The fuel and oil gauges, both the same size, are glued one to each side of the speedometer and slightly lower. Diagram 4 shows the positions of all three gauges. You will find tweezers helpful for holding and gluing these pieces.

Locate gauges as shown. Speedometer is at top center, ¼" from top edge of dashboard.

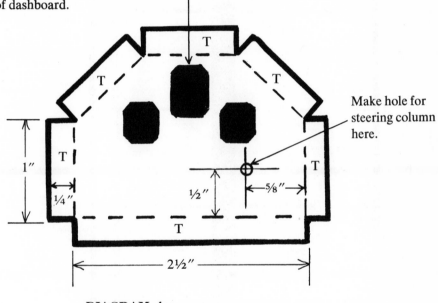

Make hole for steering column here.

DIAGRAM 4
Dashboard

Make 1 from construction paper.
Dashboard is the same size as radiator.

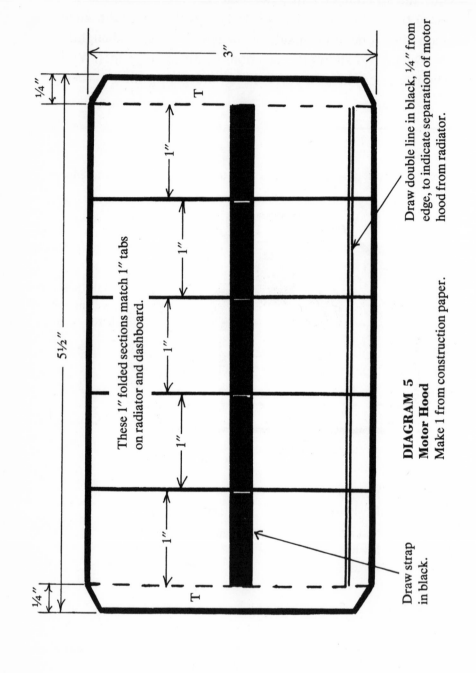

Draw double line in black, ¼″ from edge, to indicate separation of motor hood from radiator.

DIAGRAM 5
Motor Hood
Make 1 from construction paper.

These 1″ folded sections match 1″ tabs on radiator and dashboard.

Draw strap in black.

3″

5½″

¼″

¼″

1″

1″

1″

1″

1″

T

T

Motor Hood (Diagram 5)

The hood of the motor compartment is also made of construction paper; it can be the same color as the radiator and dashboard, or a different color. See diagram 5 for its shape and dimensions.

In the early days of the automobile, engine hoods were held in place by strong straps. Before folding the cut-out hood, draw the strap as shown in the diagram. Also draw the double black line with India ink or crayon near the edge of the hood (see diagram 5). Draw heavy black lines with India ink or crayon at each of the four inner fold lines. These heavy lines represent the hinged sections of the hood. Finally, fold the hood along each of its six fold lines. See the photos of the finished model on pages 60, 78, and 87.

Assembling the Motor Compartment

Begin assembling the motor compartment by gluing the radiator to the hood. It is easiest to work with your parts in an upside-down position. Place the hood flat on your work surface, strap side down and with the double line nearer to you. Put a generous amount of glue on the top gluing tab of the radiator. Turning the radiator upside-down with the grill design toward you, attach the tab to the center edge of the hood. The two sections should match perfectly if you have made the cuts and folds accurately.

Put glue on the next tab to your left, bring the corresponding section of the hood to it, and press the two sections firmly together. Then do the same for the last section of the hood and the last tab on the left side of the radiator. Follow the same procedure for gluing the tabs and sections on the right side of the radiator and hood.

Glue the dashboard to the other end of the hood in the same way. See the photos of the finished model, pages 60, 78, and 87, to see how the motor compartment should look.

67

Radiator Cap (Diagram 6)

While the motor compartment is drying, make the radiator cap. Cut a strip of yellow construction paper ¼ inch wide and 1 inch long. Roll the strip over a pencil. Press the strip firmly against the pencil as you do this to form the strip into a ring. Overlap the ends of the ring and glue them together, making a ring about ¼ inch in diameter (see diagram 6).

Cut a disc ⅜ inch in diameter from black construction paper. Glue the disc to one end of the yellow ring to finish the radiator cap as in diagram 6. Glue the completed radiator cap to the top center front of the motor compartment.

With the radiator cap firmly in place, the motor compartment is completed and ready to be attached to the chassis. Put generous amounts of glue on all the gluing tabs at the bottom of the compartment. Line up the front edge of the motor compartment with the front edge of the chassis. Line up the side edges, too. Then press downward firmly. Hold the two pieces together for a few moments until the glue sets.

Seat Compartment (Diagrams 6-7)

The seat compartment of the Mercedes model consists of three sections—two side panels and a top. Draw and cut the two side panels as shown in diagram 6. Make them from the same color construction paper as the motor compartment. Using India ink or black crayon, draw the molding on one side of each panel (see diagram 6).

Draw and cut the seat compartment top, following diagram 7. Score the dotted lines and fold carefully. Then lay the top flat and draw the molding on section #1 with India ink or black crayon. Assemble the seat compartment by gluing the top first to one side panel, then to the other. Use extra care when doing this so each of the first three numbered sections of the top matches perfectly its corresponding numbered tab on the side panels.

DIAGRAM 6

Radiator Cap

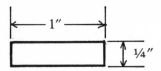

Body
Make 1 from
construction paper.

¼" diameter

Roll radiator cap
body into ring.

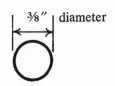

⅜" diameter

Disc
Make 1 from black
construction paper.

**Radiator Cap
Assembly**

Do not fold here. This dotted line
represents section #4 of seat
compartment top bent downward
between side panels and glued to
floor.

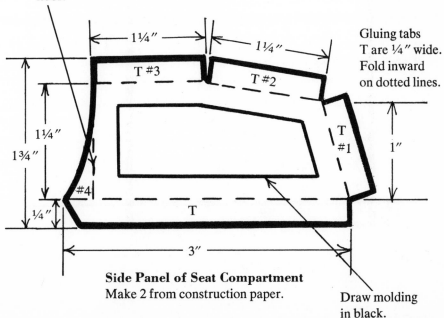

Gluing tabs
T are ¼" wide.
Fold inward
on dotted lines.

Side Panel of Seat Compartment
Make 2 from construction paper.

Draw molding
in black.

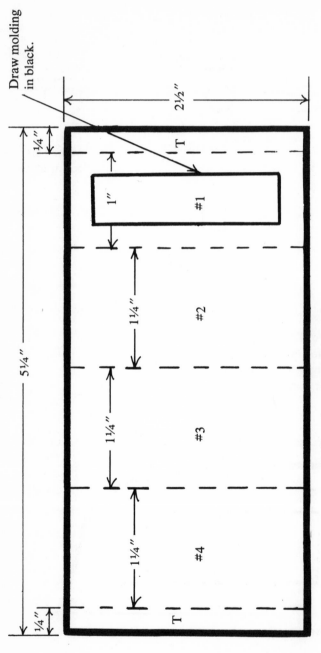

Draw molding in black.

1/4"

T

1"

#1

2 1/2"

1 1/4"

#2

5 1/4"

1 1/4"

#3

1 1/4"

#4

1/4"

T

Fold on dotted lines to match
corresponding numbered tabs on
side panels.

DIAGRAM 7
Top of Seat Compartment
Make 1 from construction paper.

The final section (#4) of the top is bent straight down inside the curved ends of the side panels; its gluing tab is attached to the floor of the car. Be sure the gluing tab is bent backward, under the seat compartment.

After the seat compartment is assembled and firmly glued, attach it to the chassis. As you did with the motor compartment, put a generous amount of glue on the bottom gluing tabs, line up the side and back edges of the compartment with the side and back edges of the chassis, and then press the two sections firmly together. Hold them in place for a few moments until the glue sets.

Cowling (Diagram 8)

The cowling is a curved section around the front of the driver's compartment. On the real Mercedes, it served to break the force of the wind while the car traveled at top speed. For your model, draw and cut the cowling as shown in diagram 8. Use construction paper of the same color as the motor and seat compartments. This piece is a bit more difficult to draw and cut than some of the others, so work with extra care. The gluing tabs are very important; do not skip any of them.

Attach the cowling by first gluing one of the long side tabs to the chassis floor. Glue the tab exactly at the edge of the chassis between the seat compartment and the dashboard. Next, glue the series of smaller tabs to the inner rim of the dashboard. Glue two tabs at a time. Do not try to do more than two because you will have trouble holding them in place while the glue dries. Finally, glue the remaining long tab to the other edge of the chassis floor. Your model will now begin to look like the Mercedes of 1904.

Seat (Diagrams 9-10)

The Mercedes model has two seats, just as the real racing car had. The one on the right was the driver's seat and the other

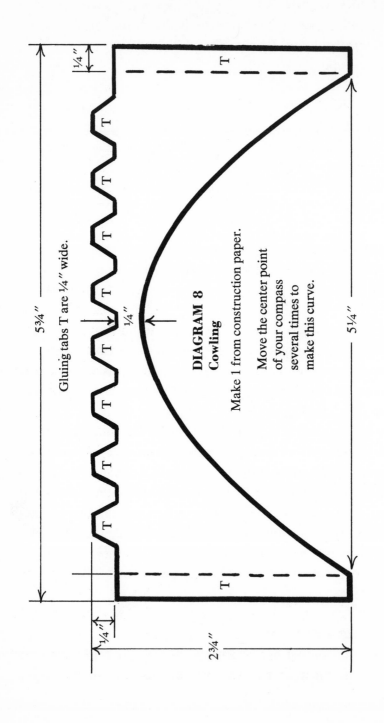

¼″

5¾″

Gluing tabs T are ¼″ wide.

T

T

T

T

T

T

T

T

¼″

¼″

2¾″

T

T

DIAGRAM 8
Cowling

Make 1 from construction paper.

Move the center point
of your compass
several times to
make this curve.

5¼″

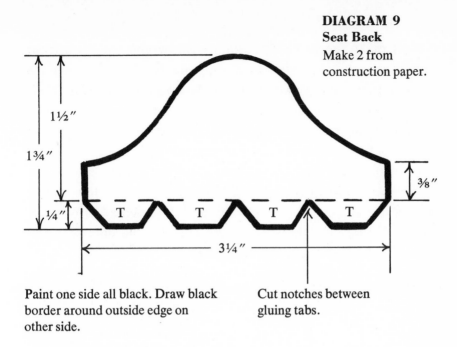

DIAGRAM 9
Seat Back
Make 2 from
construction paper.

1½″

1¾″

¼″

3¼″

⅜″

T   T   T   T

Paint one side all black. Draw black
border around outside edge on
other side.

Cut notches between
gluing tabs.

was for his mechanic helper. The two seats are probably the
most difficult parts to be made for the model. But with care and
patience, you should be able to make them without too much
trouble. Each seat consists of two sections—a back and a
cushion.

Draw and cut two seat backs as shown in diagram 9. A compass will be helpful for drawing the large curve. Use construction paper of the same color as the seat compartment, or a
different color if you prefer. Notice that the gluing tab along the
bottom of the seat back has a series of notches. These cut-outs
are needed to make the back bend more easily around the
cushion. Draw a heavy black border on the outside edge of the
seat back with pen and India ink. The inside of the seat back is
painted all black; use India ink or poster paint to do this.

The seat back is a curved piece. Curve it over the edge of
your table or a ruler, or even a thick pencil. The paper will
curve more easily if it is first slightly dampened with a sponge.
Be careful, however, not to use too much water, or the paper
will tear.

Next make the two seat cushions. Draw and cut them from yellow construction paper as in diagram 10. Lay the cushions flat and draw the cushion design as shown in the diagram. Fold the side gluing tabs down at right angles and glue them to the inner sides of the seat back. Hold the seat back against these tabs for a few moments until the glue sets.

After both seats are completed, glue them side by side to the top forward edge of the seat compartment. Use the lower edge only of the seat cushion's front tab and the notched tabs of the seat back to attach the seats to the car. See the photos of the finished model on pages 60, 78, and 87.

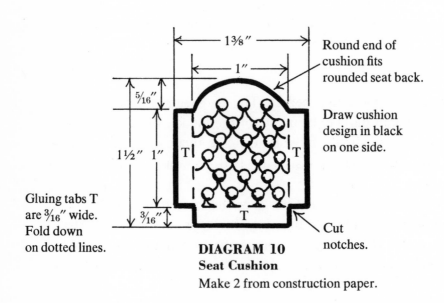

Round end of cushion fits rounded seat back.

Draw cushion design in black on one side.

Gluing tabs T are ³⁄₁₆″ wide. Fold down on dotted lines.

DIAGRAM 10
Seat Cushion
Make 2 from construction paper.

Cut notches.

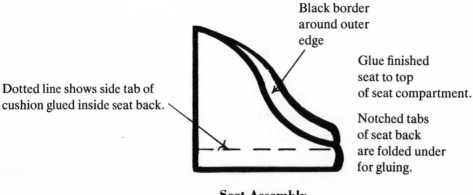

Black border around outer edge

Glue finished seat to top of seat compartment.

Dotted line shows side tab of cushion glued inside seat back.

Notched tabs of seat back are folded under for gluing.

Seat Assembly
Side View

Gas and Clutch Pedals (Diagram 11)

The gas and clutch pedals are made of rigid cardboard and pieces of wooden matchstick. Each pedal consists of a foot plate and a shaft. Use red cardboard for the foot plates, or any other color you wish. The shafts are painted yellow. See diagram 11 for the shapes and dimensions of these parts. After cutting and painting, glue the pedals to the slanted ends of the shafts.

Glue the assembled pedals to the floor of the driver's compartment. They are located side by side about 1½ inches in front of the driver's seat. Pedal A is about 1 inch from the right side of the car; pedal B is about ¾ inch from the right side (see diagram 11).

Steering Column and Steering Wheel (Diagram 12)

The steering column is made from a 4-inch length of a large wooden matchstick, as shown in diagram 12. Cut one end at an angle as shown in the diagram. Paint the column yellow, or any color you choose.

The steering wheel is made from rigid white cardboard. See diagram 12 for the size and the design to be drawn. The spoke design is drawn in black on both sides of the wheel. Use your compass for drawing the outline of the wheel as well as for the design.

Cutting the wheel in as perfect a circle as possible may prove a little difficult. If your first effort does not turn out to your satisfaction, try again. A trick to remember is to turn the piece constantly into the scissors as you cut. By doing this, you will make a better curve with fewer straight angles.

Glue the steering wheel to the straight end of the column. Place the steering wheel flat on your working surface. Put a generous amount of glue exactly in the center of the wheel. Let it stand for a few moments until the glue becomes tacky. Then press the straight end of the column into the glue, keeping the

DIAGRAM 11

Gas and Clutch Pedal
Make 2 from
rigid cardboard.

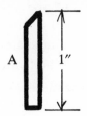

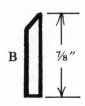

Pedal Shafts
Cut 1 of each from
large matchsticks.
Cut one end of each
shaft at an angle.

Glue pedals to
angled ends
of shafts.

Pedal Assembly

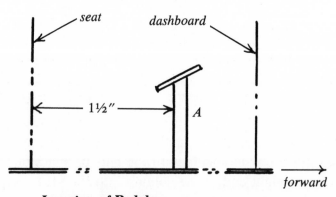

Location of Pedals
Pedal A is about 1″ from right side of
car. Pedal B is next to pedal A,
¾″ from right side of car.

DIAGRAM 12

Cut this end
at an angle.

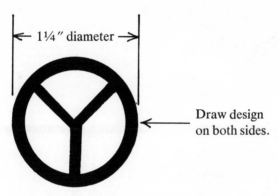

←——————— 4″ ———————→

Steering Column
Make 1 from large matchstick.

←— 1¼″ diameter —→

Draw design
on both sides.

Steering Wheel
Make 1 from rigid white cardboard.

Steering Wheel Assembly

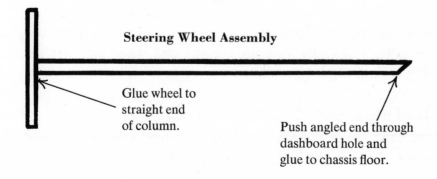

Glue wheel to
straight end
of column.

Push angled end through
dashboard hole and
glue to chassis floor.

column upright and as straight as possible. Hold it in position until it no longer leans to one side. Support the column with a small box, jar, or anything at all until the two pieces are firmly attached. Go on to make another part of the model while you wait for the steering wheel and column to dry.

To install the steering wheel and column, put glue in the hole in the dashboard as well as on the angled end of the steering column. Push the column through the hole until you feel the angled end touch the chassis behind the dashboard. The steering wheel and column should be at an angle directly in front of the driver's seat. Be sure the column and wheel are straight from front to back (see photo).

Hand Brake and Shift Rod (Diagram 13)
The hand brake and shift rod are made from lengths of round toothpicks and attached to a holder. Both are 2⅜ inches long.

78

DIAGRAM 13

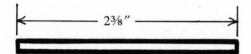

2⅜″

Hand Brake and Shift Rod
Cut 2 from round toothpicks.
Cut off pointed ends of toothpicks.

⅜″

Handle
Cut 2 from round toothpicks.
Paint black.

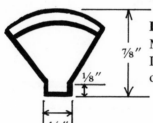

⅞″

⅛″

¼″

Holder
Make 1 from rigid cardboard.
Draw design in black
on both sides.

handles

Hand Brake and Shift Rod Assembly

Glue hand brake and shift rod to holder, one vertical and the other angled toward driver's seat.

DIAGRAM 14

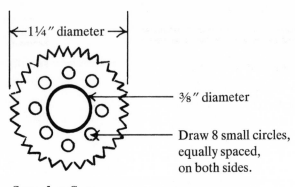

Sprocket Gear
Make 2 from rigid cardboard.

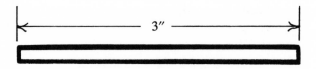

Gear Rod
Make 1 from large matchstick.

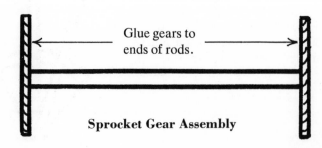

Sprocket Gear Assembly

At the top of each one there is a short ⅜-inch handle. These are also cut from round toothpicks. The hand brake and shift rod are painted yellow. The handles are painted black. Glue the handles to the ends of the hand brake and shift rod (see diagram 13).

The holder is made from rigid white cardboard. Draw and cut it as shown in diagram 13. Draw the design on both sides of the holder as shown. Then glue the hand brake and shift rod to the holder. One is attached in an upright position, the other at an angle toward the back of the car (see diagram 13). When both are firmly attached to the holder, glue the whole unit to the right side of the model, with the bottom even with the bottom edge of the chassis. See the photo for placement of the unit (page 78).

Sprocket Gears (Diagram 14)

On most of the early racing cars, the engine's power was transmitted to the rear wheels by means of sprocket gears and chains. Basically, the arrangement was similar to that of a present-day bicycle, except that a bicycle uses foot power rather than an engine.

On the Mercedes model, there are two sprocket gears and a gear rod. The gears are drawn and cut from rigid white cardboard (see diagram 14). Draw the design as shown on both sides of the gears, using India ink or black crayon. Cutting the gear teeth may present a bit of a problem, but with patience and care it can be done. Try to cut the teeth as accurately as you can, since this will add to the finished appearance of your model.

The gear rod is made from a 3-inch length of a large wooden matchstick. Paint the rod yellow with poster paint. Glue the gears to the ends of the rod one at a time, using the same upside-down method you used for gluing the steering wheel to the steering column.

81

The sprocket gear assembly is glued to the underside of the chassis 2½ inches in from the back end. Its location is approximately under the forward edge of the seat compartment. Be sure the gears extend the same distance from each side of the chassis.

Fuel Tank (Diagram 15)

The fuel tank is made of construction paper, rolled and glued into a cylinder. It can be orange or whatever color you wish. Diagram 15 shows the size and shape of the body of the tank. After you cut it out, roll the flat piece over the edge of your work table or ruler, or around a thick pencil. This will make it easier to roll the paper into a cylinder. Then bring the ends of the paper together until you have formed a cylinder approximately ¾ inch in diameter. Keep checking the cylinder opening with your ruler until it is the right size. Then glue the cylinder together at the overlapping edge. Slide a thick pencil or rod inside the cylinder; then you can run your finger back and forth over the glued edge, pressing against the pencil or rod beneath.

Close the open ends of the tank with two discs of the same color paper. Use your ruler and compass to draw and cut the discs to match the openings of the tank (see diagram 15). Glue the discs to the tank openings. If they turn out a little too large, trim off the excess paper with a small scissors. Before doing this, however, make sure the discs are firmly glued to the tank.

Two black bands are glued around the tank. On the real Mercedes these were used to fasten the tank to the racer. The two bands for the model are cut from black construction paper. Each band is ⅛ inch wide and about 2 inches long (see diagram 15). Glue the bands around the tank about ⅜ inch from each end. Cut off any excess paper if the bands are too long.

Glue the tank on the left side of the car; apply the glue along the side of the tank where the bands overlap. See the photos for placement of the fuel tank, pages 60 and 87.

DIAGRAM 15

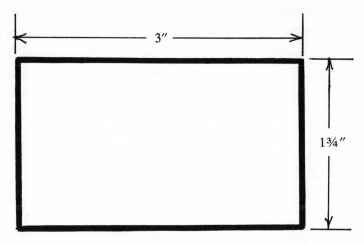

Fuel Tank
Make 1 from
construction paper.

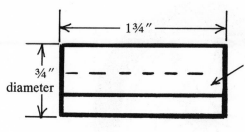

Roll tank into cylinder, ¾″ in
diameter. Overlap ends about ¼″.
Cut off excess paper if necessary.

¾″
diameter

1¾″

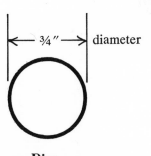

Disc
Make 2 from
construction paper.
Glue to ends of tank.

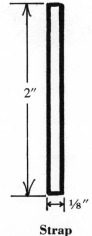

2″

⅛″

Strap
Make 2 from black
construction paper.

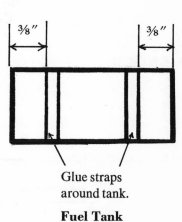

Glue straps
around tank.

**Fuel Tank
Assembly**

Wheels (Diagram 16)

The four wheels of the Mercedes model are drawn and cut from rigid cardboard. See diagram 16 for the correct dimensions and the design. Draw the tire and spoke design on both sides of each wheel with India ink, black poster paint, or black crayon. The tire outlines, rims, and hubcaps should be drawn with a compass.

Axles (Diagram 16)

Two 3¼-inch axles are needed for the Mercedes model. They are made from large wooden matchsticks. Cut the axles as shown in diagram 16 and paint them with yellow poster paint.

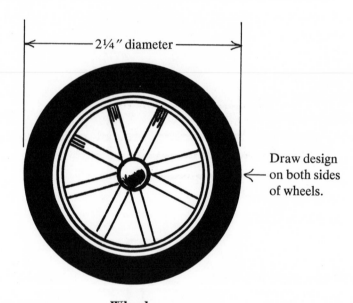

DIAGRAM 16

← 2¼″ diameter →

Draw design
← on both sides
of wheels.

Wheel
Make 4 from rigid cardboard.

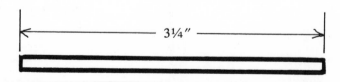

← 3¼″ →

Axle
Make 2 from large matchsticks.

Wheel Boxes (Diagram 17)

In order to glue the wheels and axles firmly together, four wheel boxes are needed. These are made of rigid cardboard and folded as shown in diagram 17. Before gluing the boxes to the wheels, cut an "X" in the center of each box with the point of your knife. The ends of the axles will be pushed through these "X" cuts, so make them large enough. One box is glued to the exact center of each wheel. This becomes the inner side of the wheel, to which the axle end is glued.

Glue the wheels to the axle ends one at a time. Place a wheel flat on your working surface, box side upward. Put a generous amount of glue on the end of the axle and thrust it firmly through the "X" part of the wheel box until it meets the center of the inner side of the wheel. Position the axle vertically, as straight as possible. The box will hold the axle until the glue dries, so you don't have to support it. Follow the same method for each of the three remaining wheels.

After the wheels are firmly attached to the axles, glue the units to the model. Position and glue the front pair of wheels at the front edge of the chassis. The rear wheels are positioned ½ inch from the rear edge of the chassis. Make sure the front and back wheels are the same distance from the sides of your racer. If the wheels are crooked, they will detract from the appearance of the model.

Sprocket Chains

Two sprocket chains are made from lengths of medium-thick string, white if possible. The length of each piece of string must be determined by the "try-and-cut" method. This means that a length of string is tried for size by holding one end of it on a rear wheel box and stretching it around the teeth of the gear and back to the wheel box. When the approximate length is found, the string is cut and glued in place.

To attach the sprocket chain, first glue one end to the wheel

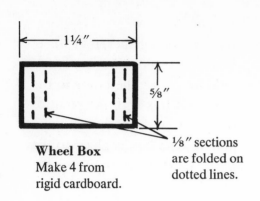

Wheel Box
Make 4 from
rigid cardboard.

1¼″

⅝″

⅛″ sections
are folded on
dotted lines.

Wheel box to look
as below when folded.

Cut "X" in
center of box.

DIAGRAM 17

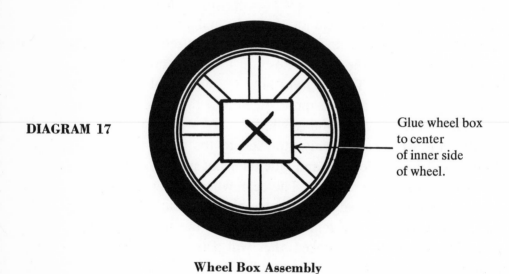

Glue wheel box
to center
of inner side
of wheel.

Wheel Box Assembly

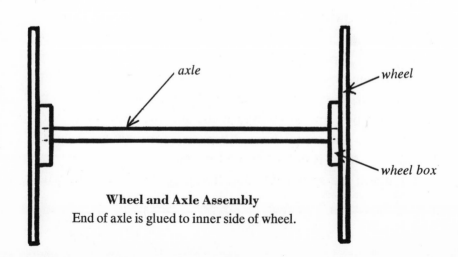

axle

wheel

wheel box

Wheel and Axle Assembly
End of axle is glued to inner side of wheel.

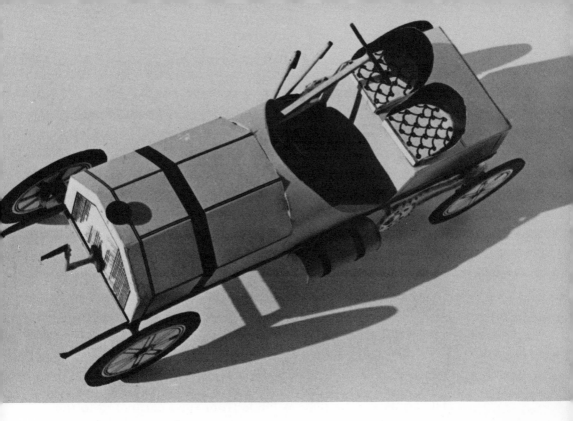

box (or to the axle if it is easier). Let the glue harden before trying to stretch the string around the teeth of the gear. While you are waiting, put a generous amount of glue on the gear teeth. The glue will be tacky by the time you are ready to bring the string over the gear, and this will make the string stick better. Again, let the glue harden before bringing the loose end of the string back to the wheel box and gluing it. Follow the same method for attaching the second sprocket chain. See the photo of the finished model.

Crank Handle (Diagram 18)

The crank handle is the last item to make for the Mercedes model. It consists of three lengths of round toothpicks and a cardboard plate. Cut the three lengths of toothpick to the dimensions shown in diagram 18. Glue them together in a zigzag fashion as shown. When the pieces are firmly glued, paint two

DIAGRAM 18

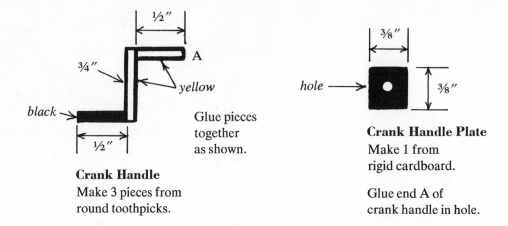

Crank Handle
Make 3 pieces from
round toothpicks.

Glue pieces together as shown.

Crank Handle Plate
Make 1 from
rigid cardboard.

Glue end A of
crank handle in hole.

of them yellow with poster paint (see diagram 18). The third length (the hand grip) is painted black with India ink or poster paint.

The crank handle plate is made from rigid cardboard to the dimensions shown in diagram 18. Drill a hole in the center of the plate with the point of your scissors or a nail. Paint one side of the plate black with India ink or poster paint.

Put a generous amount of glue in the hole of the plate. Let this stand for a few moments. Then press the yellow end of the crank handle into the hole, with the black side of the plate facing up. Hold the two pieces firmly together until they no longer move. When the crank handle and plate are firmly attached, glue the unit to the center lower edge of the radiator. The hand grip should point upward (see photo).

This will complete your Mercedes racer model and you will be ready to take on all challengers!

Duesenberg: 1921

Jimmy Murphy drove this Duesenberg racer to victory in the Le Mans Grand Prix of 1921.   INDIANAPOLIS MOTOR SPEEDWAY OFFICIAL PHOTO

The Duesenberg was a superb racing machine that made many a competitor eat its dust in the Indianapolis 500 and other track races throughout the United States in the first decades of this century. In 1921, confident that their machine could successfully challenge the best of Europe's racing cars, August and Fred Duesenberg decided to enter their racer in the Grand Prix at Le Mans, France. This classic road contest was then being revived after an interruption of seven years due mainly to World War I.

By 1921, Americans had seen a number of different European racers in road and track races. But no European had seen an American racing car. The four Duesenberg racers shipped to Le Mans were the first. Their clean, graceful lines and fine workmanship made a deep impression on car experts and spectators alike.

The Duesenbergs were powered by eight-cylinder engines, soon to become common on racing cars. Most earlier power plants consisted of four cylinders. But the Duesenbergs had one other engineering feature that set them apart from all other racing cars of the day—hydraulic brakes. A fluid of glycerine and water flowing through tubes actuated a braking mechanism on all four wheels when the driver pressed the brake pedal. The new braking system worked faster and more reliably than the usual mechanical method. Hydraulic brakes proved so superior that in a few years they became standard equipment on racing and pleasure cars.

Jimmy Murphy and three other American drivers were to handle the Duesenbergs. During a practice run over the Le Mans course, some ten miles of curves and up-and-down roadway, Murphy failed to come out of a curve properly and flipped over. He cracked several ribs but, luckily, only slightly damaged the Duesenberg. Despite his injuries Murphy was ready when race day arrived on July 25. With his ribs heavily taped, he climbed into the seat of his number 12 Duesenberg and lined up with the dozen other entries.

As the cars roared over the course, Murphy managed to keep up with the leaders. The drivers had to complete 32 laps before passing the finish flag, and it was no joy ride for any of them. Stones flew through the air as the speeding cars tore up the road surface. Tires blew or wore out on the rough road, and pit stops for repairs were frequent.

Murphy grabbed the lead as the race entered its final stage. He had roared into a commanding front position over his nearest rival when suddenly he had problems. A stone, shot from under Murphy's own wheel, ripped into the radiator. As the water leaked out, the engine overheated quickly, but

Murphy decided not to go to the pit. He would lose precious time and the end was in sight. But then, with only one lap to go, he blew a tire. Murphy now had no choice but to go to the pit.

The tire was swiftly replaced and Jimmy Murphy got back on the track still holding a slim lead. His Duesenberg was now in bad trouble because of the overheated engine, and Murphy began to have doubts about finishing. Glancing nervously over his shoulder and moving at a snail's pace, Murphy managed to limp across the finish line seconds ahead of his closest challenger driving a French car. It was the first time an American racing-car driver at the wheel of an American car had won a European racing classic.

The model you will build is the 1921 Duesenberg in which Jimmy Murphy won at Le Mans.

BUILDING THE DUESENBERG MODEL

Chassis (Diagram 1)

On rigid cardboard, draw a rectangle 2 inches wide and 7¾ inches long. Cut it out with your scissors or a knife, whichever is easier.

Draw and cut two strips, also from rigid cardboard, ¼ inch wide and 9 inches long. Cut one end of each strip in a curve (see diagram 1). These curved ends will form the front of the model.

Glue the strips edgewise along each 7¾-inch edge of the chassis. Make sure the curved edges face upward, and the straight ends of the strips are even with the back end of the chassis (see diagram 1). Finally, paint the attached chassis strips black with India ink or poster paint.

Bulkheads #1, #2, and #3 (Diagrams 2-3)

The body is the main part of the Duesenberg model and perhaps the most difficult to make. It consists of several bulkheads and

body-covering pieces. If you read the directions carefully and study the diagrams, you should be able to build it with no major problems.

Bulkheads are upright partitions within the body of the model that help give it shape and rigidity. Six bulkheads are to be drawn and cut from rigid cardboard.

Bulkhead #1 is drawn and cut as shown in diagram 2. Try to be accurate when cutting the rounded corners. This will add to the appearance of your finished model.

Bulkhead #2 is drawn and cut according to diagram 2. It is slightly wider than bulkhead #1.

Bulkhead #3 is drawn and cut according to diagram 3. This bulkhead is slightly larger than the first two and has a curved top edge. Bulkhead #3 will become the dashboard of the model; make the hole in it as indicated on diagram 3.

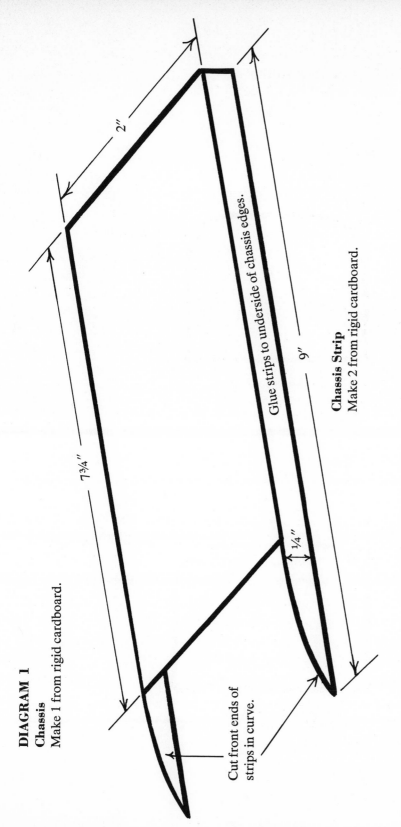

DIAGRAM 1
Chassis
Make 1 from rigid cardboard.

2"

7¾"

Glue strips to underside of chassis edges.

9"

Chassis Strip
Make 2 from rigid cardboard.

¼"

Cut front ends of strips in curve.

Note: This diagram is not to scale. Draw and cut the chassis and chassis strips to the measurements given.

DIAGRAM 2

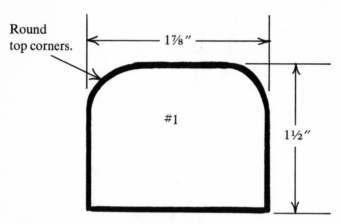

Round top corners.

1⅞″

#1

1½″

Bulkhead #1
Make 1 from
rigid cardboard.

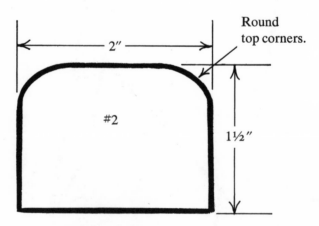

2″

Round top corners.

#2

1½″

Bulkhead #2
Make 1 from
rigid cardboard.

DIAGRAM 3

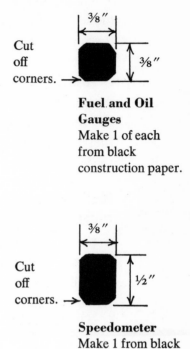

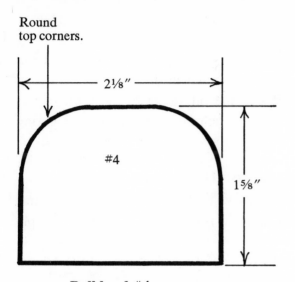

Round top corners.

2⅛″

#4

1⅝″

Bulkhead #4
Make 1 from
rigid cardboard.

⅜″

⅜″

Cut
off
corners. →

**Fuel and Oil
Gauges**
Make 1 of each
from black
construction paper.

⅜″

½″

Cut
off
corners. →

Speedometer
Make 1 from black
construction paper.

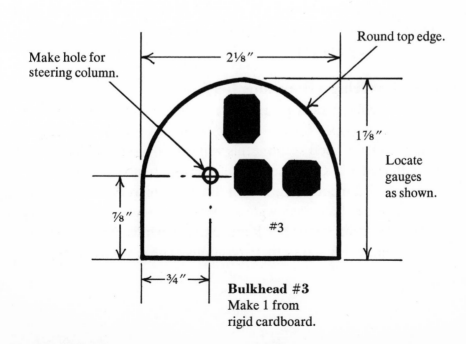

Make hole for
steering column.

Round top edge.

2⅛″

1⅞″

Locate
gauges
as shown.

⅞″

#3

¾″

Bulkhead #3
Make 1 from
rigid cardboard.

Gauges (Diagram 3)

Three gauges are to be made and installed on the Duesenberg model—a fuel gauge, an oil gauge, and a speedometer. All three are made from black construction paper. See diagram 3 for their sizes and shapes.

Attach the speedometer first; glue it to the top center of the dashboard (bulkhead #3) as shown in diagram 3. Then glue the fuel gauge below it and the oil gauge to the right of the fuel gauge. Tweezers will be helpful for placing and gluing these small parts.

Bulkheads #4, #5, and #6 (Diagrams 3-5)

Bulkheads #4 and #5 are drawn and cut according to diagrams 3 and 4. Note that bulkhead #5 is the smallest and has sharply curved top corners.

Bulkhead #6 is completely different from any of the others. Draw and cut it as shown in diagram 4.

All the bulkheads are glued upright to the top side of the chassis at the points shown in diagram 5. Bulkhead #6 is glued at right angles to the others; it extends from bulkhead #4 to the back end of the chassis. Bulkhead #5 is cut in half and glued on each side of bulkhead #6, ¾ inch in from the back end of the chassis. When gluing the bulkheads, make certain that they are all exactly upright.

Body Covering (Diagrams 6-9)

The Duesenberg racing cars were white; therefore, use white construction paper for the body covering of the model. Begin with the motor hood section; this will extend from bulkhead #1 to bulkhead #2. Cut a section of construction paper 3 inches wide and 5½ inches long. Lay it flat on your work table. Draw two black bands ³⁄₁₆ inch wide across the 5½-inch length of the paper; use India ink or black crayon. The bands are 1¼ inches apart; diagram 6 shows their positions. These bands represent

DIAGRAM 4

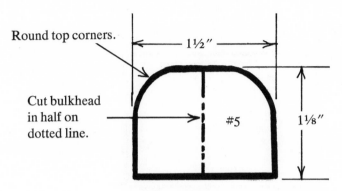

Round top corners.

Cut bulkhead
in half on
dotted line.

1½″

#5

1⅛″

Bulkhead #5
Make 1 from rigid cardboard.

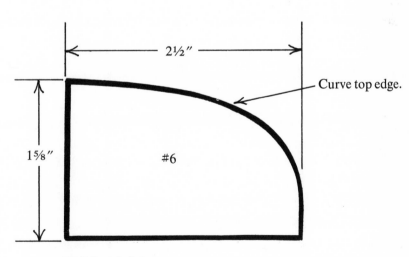

2½″

Curve top edge.

1⅝″

#6

Bulkhead #6
Make 1 from rigid cardboard.

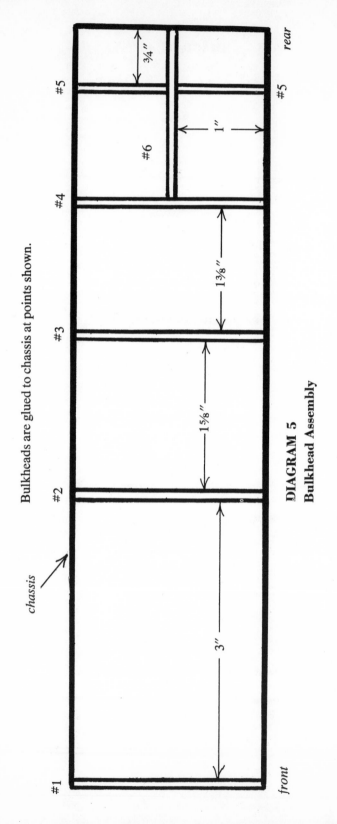

Bulkheads are glued to chassis at points shown.

DIAGRAM 5
Bulkhead Assembly

Note: This diagram is not to scale.

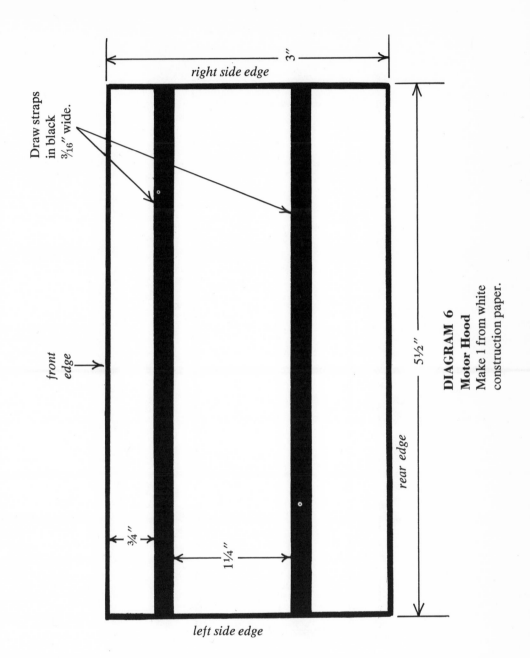

Draw straps
in black
³⁄₁₆" wide.

right side edge

3"

*front
edge*

³⁄₄"

1¼"

left side edge

5½"

rear edge

DIAGRAM 6
Motor Hood
Make 1 from white
construction paper.

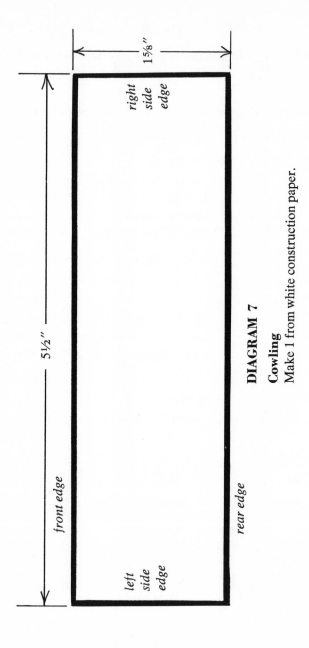

left side edge

right side edge

front edge

rear edge

5½"

1⅝"

DIAGRAM 7
Cowling
Make 1 from white construction paper.

straps that were used on the real racer to hold the motor hood securely in place.

To attach the hood, put a generous amount of glue along the edges of bulkheads #1 and #2 and along the edges of the chassis between these two bulkheads. Now press one 3-inch end of the motor hood against the chassis edge and the lower edges of the bulkheads. Make sure the strap closer to the edge of the hood is at the front of the model.

When you feel that this first portion of the hood is securely attached, continue with the rest of it, gluing one section at a time. After the motor hood is completely glued and you have reached the other edge of the chassis, there may be excess hood paper. Trim it off with a sharp knife or scissors.

The next section of the body covering is the cowling, between bulkheads #2 and #3. Cut it from white construction paper, making it 1⅝ inches wide and 5½ inches long (see diagram 7). Attach the cowling the same way you attached the motor hood. Glue one 1⅝-inch end to one side edge of the chassis, and work over the edges of the bulkheads a section at a time. Again, after reaching the other side of the chassis, cut off any excess paper.

The third body-covering section is completely different from the first two. It fits around the driver's cockpit. Draw and cut the cockpit cover as shown in diagram 8. After cutting out the cover carefully, lay it flat on your work table and draw the black border around the curved edge as shown in the diagram. Use India ink or black crayon.

Since the cockpit cover has a difficult bend, it will be helpful to slide it over the edge of your table or ruler. This will bend the cover and make it easier to glue.

To attach the cockpit cover, first glue one of the long gluing tabs to the chassis floor. When this is firm, glue the adjacent short tab to the inner or cockpit side of the dashboard.

After these tabs are secure, bend and glue the cockpit cover

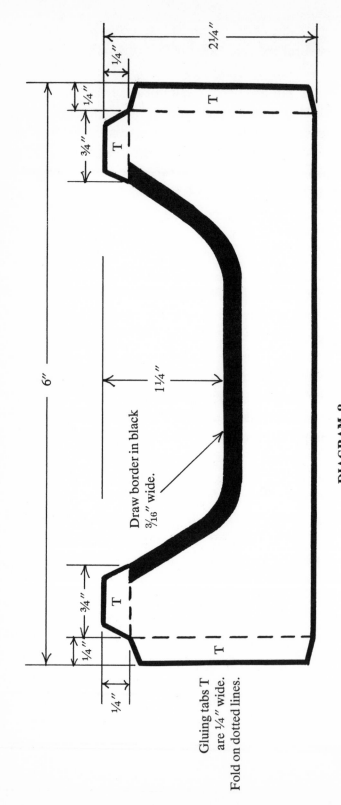

DIAGRAM 8
Cockpit Cover
Make 1 from white construction paper.

along the edge of bulkhead #4, which forms the back of the driver's seat. Now attach the second long gluing tab to the chassis floor on the opposite side of the cockpit. Finally, glue the second short tab to the inner side of the dashboard.

The fourth section of the body covering is for the tail end of the model. This may prove a little difficult to attach, but with patience you should be able to do it. The tail covering is made in two parts—a top and a bottom section. Draw and cut the top section as shown in diagram 9. This is fitted and attached first. Because of the piece's unusual shape and its complex bends, the procedure for attaching it is a "try-and-fit" method. If the section fits on your first try and looks reasonably good, fine. If not, cut and fit another piece until you are satisfied.

Gluing the top tail section involves bending it over more than one series of curves. While bending the paper one way and gluing, you will also have to bend and glue it in another direction. To help fit these compound curves, dampen the paper before trying to bend and glue it. However, be careful not to make the paper too wet, or it will be likely to tear. You may find it easiest to start gluing the section at the top of the driver's cockpit (bulkhead #4), then work down along the top edges of bulkheads #6 and #5. Finish by gluing the section to the sides of bulkheads #4 and #5.

Now draw and cut the bottom section of the tail covering. This is simply a long rectangular piece, as shown in diagram 9, that is fitted all around the bottom of the tail end. It covers the opening in the tail that remains after the top section is attached.

Start gluing this bottom strip at one side of bulkhead #4. Continue to glue it a section at a time around the edge of the chassis and along the bottom edge of the top section. Overlap a small portion of the top section. Run the bottom strip around the extreme end of the tail, gluing it to the exposed part of bulkhead #6, and then along the other side to the opposite edge of bulkhead #4. This will complete the body covering of the Duesenberg model.

DIAGRAM 9

Note: This diagram is not to scale. Draw the tail cover sections to the dimensions given.

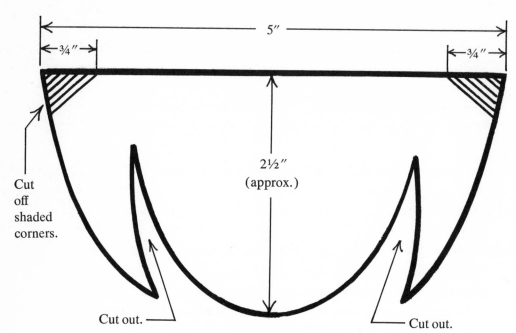

Cut off shaded corners.

Cut out.

Cut out.

Top Section of Tail Cover
Make 1 from white construction paper.

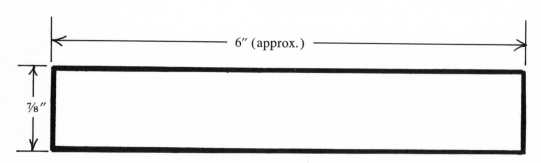

Bottom Section of Tail Cover
Make 1 from white construction paper.

Driver's Seat (Diagram 10)

Making and attaching the driver's seat will be a simple task after wrestling with the body covering! Draw and cut the seat as shown in diagram 10; use any color construction paper you wish. Fold all dotted lines accurately so the seat will look straight and pleasing to the eye—to say nothing of being comfortable for the driver!

Glue the back part of the seat first to the back portion of the driver's cockpit; this is the exposed side of bulkhead #4. Next glue the side tabs T to both sides of the cockpit. The last gluing tab is attached to the floor; make sure you bend it under the seat.

Exhaust Pipe and Muffler (Diagram 11)

The exhaust unit of the Duesenberg is made up of two sections —a muffler and the exhaust pipe itself. The latter is simply a

DIAGRAM 10

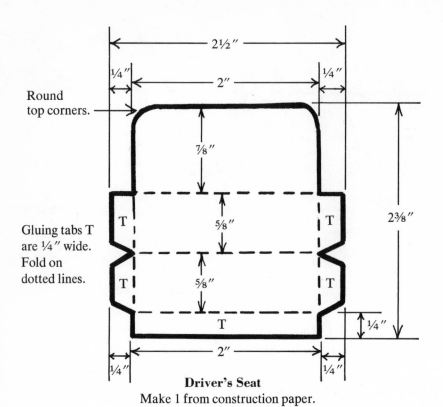

Round
top corners.

2½″

¼″ 2″ ¼″

⅞″

Gluing tabs T
are ¼″ wide.
Fold on
dotted lines.

T T
⅝″

T T
⅝″

T

2⅜″

¼″

2″

¼″ ¼″

Driver's Seat
Make 1 from construction paper.

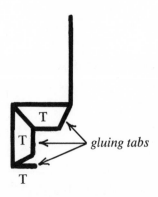

Driver's seat to look
as above when folded.

Note: This diagram is not to scale. Cut the straw to the measurement given.

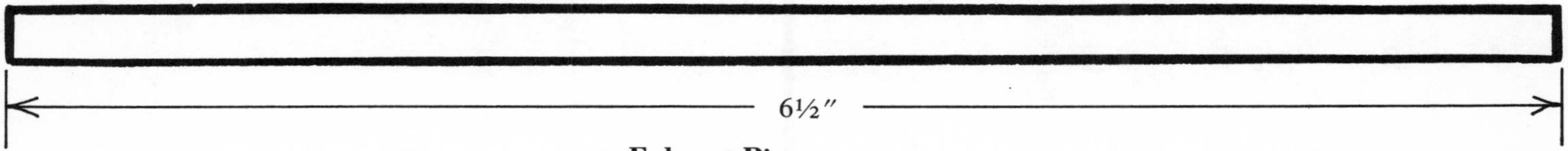

DIAGRAM 11

Exhaust Pipe
Make 1 from drinking straw.

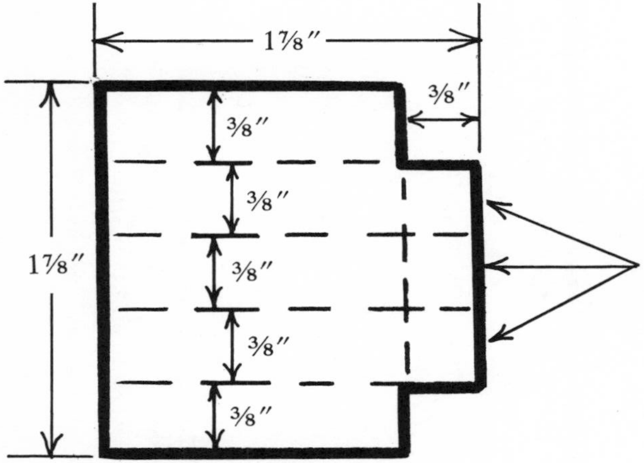

6½"

Muffler Assembly

open end

When these 3 tabs
are folded and glued,
this end of muffler
will be closed.

⅜"

1⅞"

⅜" ⅜" ⅜" ⅜" ⅜"

1⅞"

Muffler
Make 1 from construction paper.

Exhaust Unit Assembly

drinking straw cut to 6½ inches (see diagram 11). Paint the exhaust pipe if you wish—silver, black, or any other color. Or you can leave it as is, provided its design is not too gaudy.

The muffler is drawn and cut from black or blue construction paper to the dimensions given in diagram 11. Make all the folds as straight as possible; otherwise the muffler will be crooked and will detract from the finished model's appearance.

When the muffler is glued together, one end is open and the other end closed (see diagram 11). The straw is inserted into the open end and glued. After the two pieces are firmly joined, glue the exhaust unit to the right side of the car's body. The muffler should be on the side of the motor hood. See the photos, pages 92 and 105, for placement of the exhaust pipe.

Radiator Grill (Diagram 12)

The radiator grill is a separate piece on which a grill design is drawn with India ink or black crayon. Draw and cut the grill from white paper, following the dimensions given in diagram 12. Then glue it to the front end of the motor compartment.

Radiator Cap (Diagram 12)

The radiator cap consists of three pieces—a short length cut from a drinking straw and two discs cut from rigid cardboard. See diagram 12 for the correct sizes of all three pieces. You can use any color cardboard you wish for the discs, or you can color all the pieces with poster paint or crayons.

Glue the discs and straw section together as shown in diagram 12. The finished radiator cap is glued to the top front end of the motor compartment (see the photos of the finished model for placement).

Wheels (Diagram 13)

The four wheels of the Duesenberg model are 2 inches in diameter and cut from rigid cardboard. Use your compass to

DIAGRAM 12

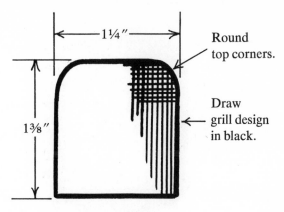

|← 1¼″ →|

1⅜″

Round
top corners.

Draw
grill design
in black.

Radiator Grill
Make 1 from construction paper.

|← ¼″ →|

Radiator Cap
Make 1 from
drinking straw.

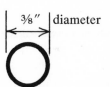

⅜″ | diameter

Disc
Make 2 from
rigid cardboard.

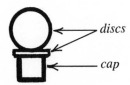

discs

cap

Radiator Cap Assembly

DIAGRAM 13

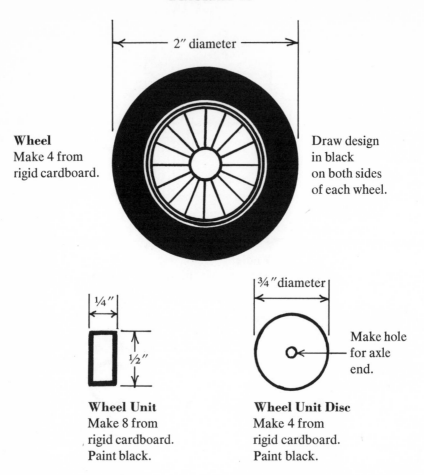

Wheel
Make 4 from
rigid cardboard.

2″ diameter

Draw design
in black
on both sides
of each wheel.

¼″

½″

¾″ diameter

Make hole
for axle
end.

Wheel Unit
Make 8 from
rigid cardboard.
Paint black.

Wheel Unit Disc
Make 4 from
rigid cardboard.
Paint black.

make the necessary circles. By pressing as hard as possible
when drawing the 2-inch circle, you will make an impression
in the cardboard that will help when you cut the piece out.
Remember while cutting to turn the piece continuously into
the scissors; this will make the wheel rounder, with few flat
lengths along the rim.

Draw the design as shown in diagram 13 on both sides of
each wheel with India ink or black crayon.

110

A small unit for the inside of each wheel is needed to attach the axles. Each of the four units is made of three pieces of rigid cardboard—two ½-inch lengths and one disc ¾ inch in diameter. See diagram 13 for drawing and cutting these pieces. Paint the units black, using India ink or poster paint.

The two straight pieces are glued parallel to one another and about ¼ inch apart on each side of the center of each wheel (see diagram 14). The disc is then glued on top of these two pieces. Before gluing the disc, however, drill a hole in its center with a nail or other sharp pointed tool. Enlarge the hole by twirling a pencil point in it so it is large enough for the axle end to fit through. (The axles are made from large wooden matchsticks.)

Attach one wheel unit to each of the four wheels. See diagram 14 to see how the finished units should look.

Wheel and Axle Assembly (Diagram 14)

The two axles of the Duesenberg racer are 3¾ inches long. Cut them from large matchsticks and paint them black with India ink or poster paint.

Put a generous amount of glue in the holes of the wheel units, and then push the ends of the axles into the holes until they meet the wheels. It is very important to do this carefully, keeping the wheels at perfect right angles to the axles. If they slant even a little, the crookedness will be very noticeable and will detract from the appearance of the finished model. See diagram 14 for the wheel and axle assembly.

The assembled wheels and axles are glued to the underside of the chassis. The front set of wheels is positioned ¼ inch in from the front end. The rear set of wheels is located 1⅝ inches in from the tail end. The wheels must be absolutely straight in relation to the sides of the chassis. Once the wheels are attached, your model will begin to look like a finished racing car.

DIAGRAM 14

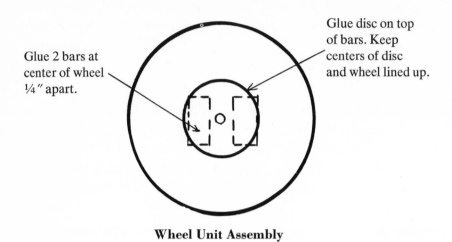

Glue 2 bars at center of wheel ¼″ apart.

Glue disc on top of bars. Keep centers of disc and wheel lined up.

Wheel Unit Assembly

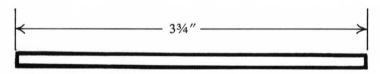

3¾″

Axle
Make 2 from large matchsticks.
Paint black.

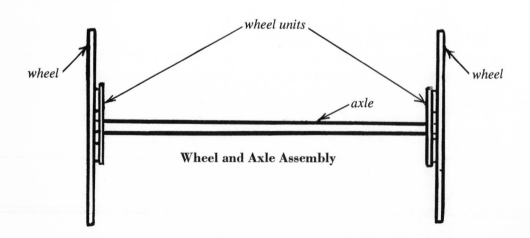

wheel units

wheel

wheel

axle

Wheel and Axle Assembly

Steering Wheel (Diagram 15)

The steering wheel is made of two pieces—a steering column and the wheel itself. The steering column is a 2-inch length of a large matchstick. One end is cut at an angle (see diagram 15). Paint the column blue or red with poster paint.

The steering wheel is cut from rigid white cardboard; it is 1¼ inches in diameter. Diagram 15 shows the design to draw on both sides of it; use India ink.

Glue the steering wheel to the angled end of the steering column. After the two pieces are firmly joined, glue the unit to the model. Put a generous amount of glue on the end of the steering column and up about half its length. Push the column through the hole in the dashboard (bulkhead #3) until the end of the column touches the chassis floor. Hold the unit for a few moments until the glue sets.

Gas Pedal and Brake Pedal (Diagrams 15-16)

The gas and brake pedals are each made of two pieces of rigid cardboard. See diagrams 15 and 16 for the sizes and shapes of the pieces for each one. Paint all the pieces black with poster paint. Then glue the pieces of each pedal together as shown in the diagrams.

Glue both pedals to the floor of the driver's cockpit and to the bottom part of the dashboard. The long side of each pedal is attached to the floor, the short side to the dashboard. Use tweezers to hold the pedals while gluing, since the space is cramped. The brake pedal (the wider one) is attached to the floor almost beneath the steering column. The narrower gas pedal is glued about ¼ inch to the right of the brake. See diagram 16 for correct location of the pedals.

Hand Brake and Shift Stick (Diagram 16)

The hand brake and shift stick are sections of round toothpicks set in a holder made from construction paper. See diagram 16

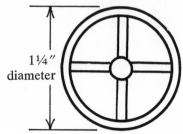

|← — — — 2″ — — — →|

Steering Column
Make 1 from large matchstick.
Paint red or blue.
Cut one end at angle.

Draw design in black
on both sides.

1¼″
diameter

Steering Wheel
Make 1 from rigid
white cardboard.

Steering Wheel Assembly

DIAGRAM 15

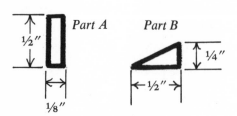

½″   *Part A*   *Part B*   ¼″

⅛″   ←½″→

A   ↓   ← B

Gas Pedal Assembly

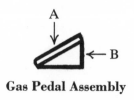

Gas Pedal
Make 1 of each part
from rigid cardboard.
Paint black.

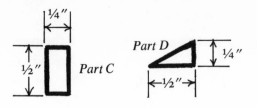

Part D

Part C

¼"

½"

¼"

½"

Brake Pedal
Make 1 of each part
from rigid cardboard.
Paint black.

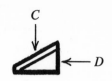

C

D

Brake Pedal Assembly

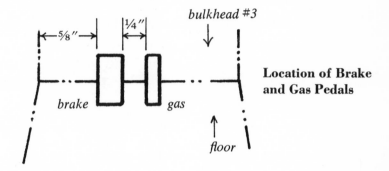

bulkhead #3

5/8"

¼"

brake

gas

floor

**Location of Brake
and Gas Pedals**

DIAGRAM 16

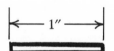

1"

Shift Stick
Make 1 from
round toothpick.
Paint black.

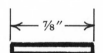

⅞"

Hand Brake
Make 1 from
round toothpick.
Paint black.

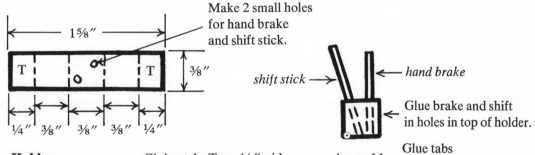

Make 2 small holes
for hand brake
and shift stick.

1⅝"

3/8"

T

T

¼"   3/8"   3/8"   3/8"   ¼"

Holder
Make 1 from
construction paper.

Gluing tabs T are ¼" wide.
Fold on dotted lines
to form a box shape.

shift stick →

← hand brake

Assembly

← Glue brake and shift
in holes in top of holder.

Glue tabs
to floor
of chassis.

for the size and shape of the holder and the lengths of the hand brake and shift stick. The diagram also shows how the holder is folded and the whole unit is glued together. The shorter upright hand brake should be in front and to the right of the longer shift stick, which is set at an angle.

When it is assembled, the unit is glued to the floor of the driver's cockpit just to the right of the gas pedal.

Windshield (Diagram 17)

The Duesenberg racer was equipped with a wire-mesh windshield to protect the driver from flying stones. On dirt tracks or country roads, stones were sent flying backward like bullets by the spinning wheels of the racers. The windshield for your model is made of white construction paper with the mesh design drawn on both sides with India ink or black crayon. See diagram 17 for the shape and size of the windshield.

The windshield is glued on top of the cowling, directly in front of the driver's position. The photo of the finished model shows the location of the windshield.

Crank Handle (Diagram 17)

The Duesenberg racer did not have a self-starter; a crank handle was used to start the engine. This had to be turned around several times before the engine caught and roared into action. It took a good strong arm to do the cranking!

For the model, the crank handle is made of three pieces of round toothpicks. These are cut to the lengths shown in diagram 17 and assembled. After the pieces are firmly glued together, paint the entire crank handle black with India ink or poster paint.

The crank handle is glued to the bottom center part of the radiator (see the photo of the finished model). Make a hole in the radiator with a nail or other pointed tool. Put a generous

116

amount of glue on the end of the long 1¼-inch piece (part C).
Push this halfway into the hole with the handle in an up
position.

Numbers (Diagram 17)

Draw and cut three sets of the number 12, two sets black and
one set white. Use white construction paper for the white set,
and black construction paper or black paint on white construction paper for the black sets. See diagram 17 for the style of
the numbers.

Glue the white 12 to the front of the radiator. The black
numbers are glued to the right and left sides of the model,
slightly in front of the driver's cockpit. See the photo of the
finished model for location of the numbers.

117

DIAGRAM 17

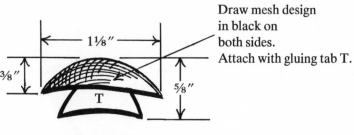

Draw mesh design
in black on
both sides.
Attach with gluing tab T.

1⅛″

⅜″

⅝″

T

Windshield
Make 1 from white
construction paper.

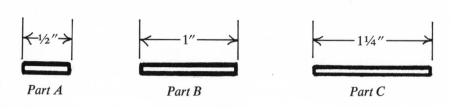

←½″→

←1″→

←1¼″→

Part A

Part B

Part C

Crank Handle
Make 1 of each part from round toothpicks.
Paint black.

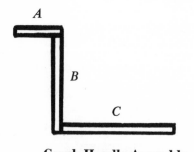

A

B

C

Crank Handle Assembly
Glue end of part C
in hole in bottom of radiator.

⅞″

Number
Make 2 sets from black
construction paper.

Make 1 set from white
construction paper.

Front Wheel Stabilizers (Diagram 18)

Stabilizers were attached to the front wheels of the Duesenberg racer to help the driver control his car at high speeds and especially around curves.

For the model, the front wheel stabilizers are made from large matchsticks. See diagram 18 for the lengths to be cut. Make sure when assembling each stabilizer that the short ½-inch length is attached at right angles to the others. Of course, these pieces must point in opposite directions on right and left sides; see diagram 18 and the photo on page 117 for help with these parts.

After assembling both stabilizers, paint them black with India ink or poster paint. Then glue the long end of each one to the front axle, and glue the ½-inch right-angled end to the chassis.

DIAGRAM 18

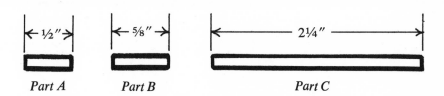

Part A   Part B   Part C

Front Wheel Stabilizer
Make 2 of each part from large matchsticks. Paint black.

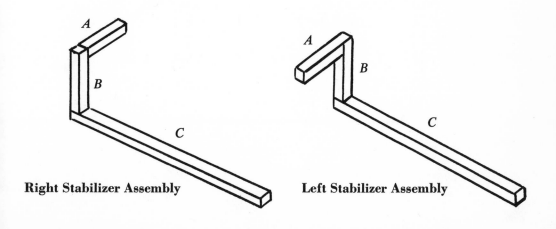

Right Stabilizer Assembly   **Left Stabilizer Assembly**

Flag

A small American flag is attached to the tail end of the Duesenberg model, to the left of and slightly behind the driver's cockpit. You may draw a flag separately and glue it to the racer; do not make it larger than 1¼ inches by ⅞ inch. Or, if you want the flag to look more realistic, you can buy one in a hobby shop or stationery store.

Attaching the flag will complete your model of the Duesenberg racer. Then sit back and enjoy the admiring words from your friends when they see it.

Maserati: 1957

Fangio, at the wheel of his Maserati, hugs the inside edge of a curve on the Nürburgring Grand Prix course in West Germany. THE BRITISH PETROLEUM CO., LTD.

The Maserati was one of the great racing cars of the 1950s. Designed and built by Italian automotive engineers for Grand Prix competition, the Maserati proved a consistent winner throughout Europe. During the period of its popularity, the Maserati played a leading role in the development of highly specialized racing cars. It pioneered many new features relating to engines, acceleration, brakes, and suspension, among others.

The Nürburgring Grand Prix of 1957 in West Germany was probably the most memorable race in which the Maserati was involved. The hills, downgrades, and innumerable twisting curves of this 14-mile road course make it one of the most difficult in the world for Grand Prix racing. Drivers had to complete a little more than 22 laps around the route before passing the checkered finish flag. For this particular race the Maserati was driven by the brilliant Juan Manuel Fangio of Argentina, five-time winner of the World Championship of Drivers.

It was a star-filled field of drivers on that August 4th race day at Nürburgring. But the crowd knew there were three standouts to be watched more than the others. Aside from Fangio, they were Mike Hawthorn and Peter Collins, two young racing stars from Great Britain. Both were driving Ferraris, another superb Italian racer. As the end of the race approached, these three had boomed their way far in front of the pack.

Hawthorn, Collins, and Fangio were bunched in that order as the last two laps came up. The veteran Argentinian had been biding his time, but as lap 21 began, he was ready to make his move. His first task was to overtake Peter Collins in second position.

The drivers whizzed past the grandstand. Fangio pressed harder on the accelerator. Collins shot a glance at his rear view mirror and saw the Maserati's nose slowly edging past him. Fangio slid into the second spot.

But Collins wasn't through yet. He gave his Ferrari an extra burst of gas and regained second place. Then, as the racers came to a curve, Fangio took it full tilt; Collins slowed just a trifle. In that instant Fangio flashed by the Englishman once more. A hail of stones shot from beneath Fangio's rear wheels. Some flew up and shattered Collins's goggles. Momentarily blinded, he ripped off the damaged goggles and, in a reflex action, let up on the accelerator. At that moment Peter Collins was out of the race.

Fangio now bent to the job of catching Mike Hawthorn. Just as he had done with Collins, he moved up closer and closer. The Argentinian was daring to the point of recklessness as he shot around curves without slowing his speed. His all-out driving tactics brought results. He caught and passed Hawthorn along the back stretches of the course.

As the drivers roared past the grandstand for the final time, Fangio was leading by not much more than a car length. The skilled veteran used every trick he knew to hold his front spot. When the checkered flag fell, he had widened the gap between himself and Hawthorn to almost three car lengths.

The Nürburgring Grand Prix of 1957 proved to be Fangio's dramatic goodbye to racing. At the end of that season he announced his retirement from the sport.

The Maserati model is based on the car Fangio drove to victory at Nürburgring. If the work is done with care and patience, it will prove to be an extremely handsome addition to your collection.

BUILDING THE MASERATI MODEL

Chassis (Diagram 1)

The chassis of the Maserati model is drawn and cut from rigid cardboard. Follow the dimensions given in diagram 1.

Bulkheads (Diagrams 2-3)

In order to properly shape the body of the Maserati, it is necessary to attach a series of bulkheads to the chassis. Most of the bulkheads have different shapes, as you can see from the diagrams. Draw and cut all six bulkheads from rigid cardboard, following the diagrams.

Make certain when gluing the bulkheads to the chassis that you keep them in a perfectly upright position. Otherwise you will have difficulty gluing the body covering to them. See diagram 4 for their proper placement.

Bulkhead #4 is quite different from the first three. Draw and cut this bulkhead with extra care in order to shape the racer's tail correctly. Bulkhead #4 also provides the back part of the driver's compartment.

Bulkhead #5 is another quite different pattern. It forms the spine of the racer's tail end. Draw and cut it with care. As you

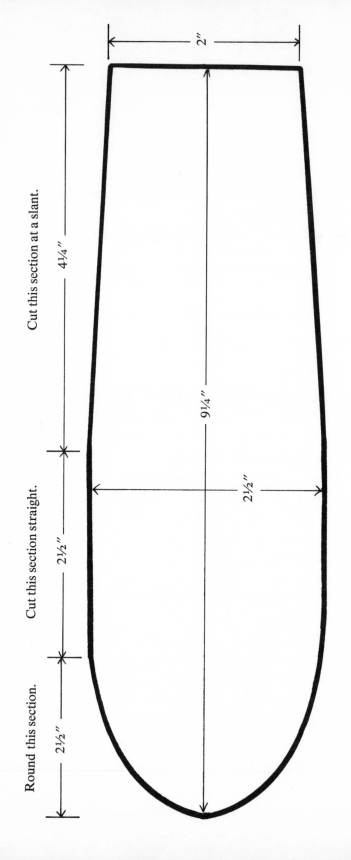

Cut this section at a slant.

4¼"

Cut this section straight.

2½"

Round this section.

2½"

2"

9¼"

2½"

DIAGRAM 1

Chassis

Make 1 from rigid cardboard.

Note: This diagram is not to scale. Draw the chassis to the measurements given.

DIAGRAM 2

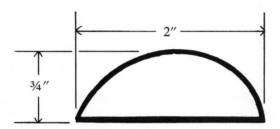

Bulkhead #1
Make 1 from rigid cardboard.

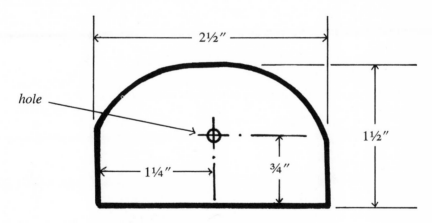

hole

Bulkheads #2 and #3
Make 2 this size from rigid cardboard.

Make hole only in bulkhead #3 for steering column.

DIAGRAM 3

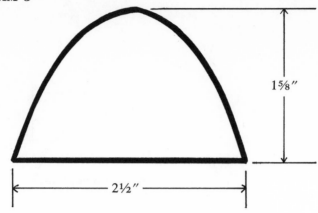

Bulkhead #4
Make 1 from rigid cardboard.

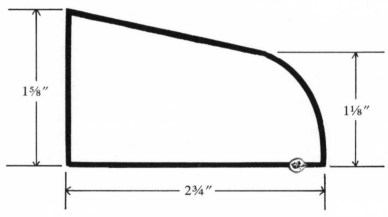

Bulkhead #5
Make 1 from rigid cardboard.

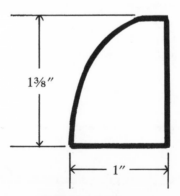

Bulkhead #6
Make 2 from rigid cardboard.

DIAGRAM 4

Location of Bulkheads

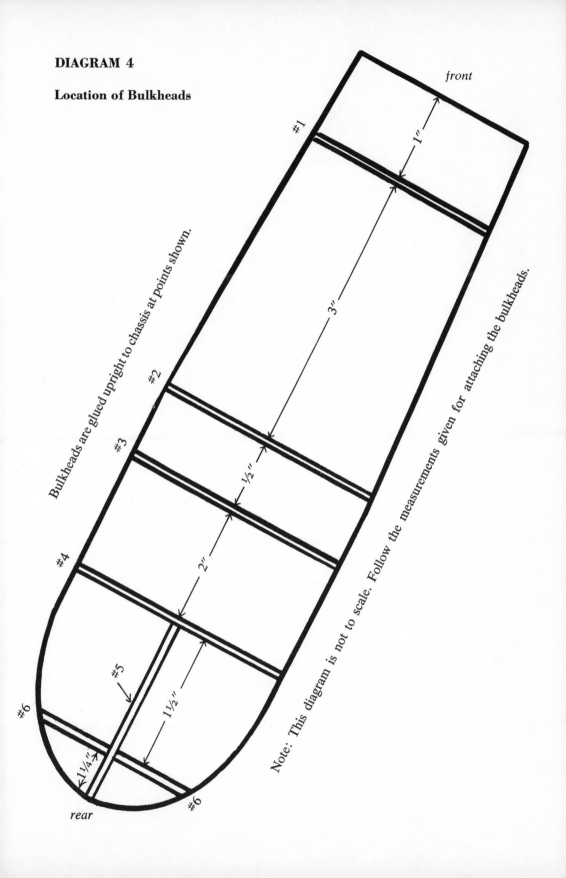

front

#1

1″

3″

#2

½″

#3

2″

#4

#5

1½″

#6

1¼″

#6

rear

Bulkheads are glued upright to chassis at points shown.

Note: This diagram is not to scale. Follow the measurements given for attaching the bulkheads.

see in diagram 4, this bulkhead is glued at right angles to bulkhead #4, along the center of the chassis. The end of bulkhead #5 should meet the tail end of the chassis.

Notice that bulkhead #6 is made in two parts. Glue them at right angles to bulkhead #5, about 1½ inches behind bulkhead #4. Diagram 4 shows the placement of all six bulkheads.

Radiator (Diagram 5)

After all the bulkheads are firmly in place, draw and cut the radiator. Use white construction paper for making the radiator, and draw it as shown in diagram 5. Draw the grill design on one side with India ink or black crayon. Glue the radiator ⅛ inch in from the front end of the chassis. Be sure you attach it in a perfectly upright position.

128

Motor Hood (Diagram 5)

The motor hood and the rest of the Maserati's body covering are made of the same color construction paper; use any color you wish. While this paper is rather fragile and must be handled carefully, it has the advantage of being easily shaped for difficult curves.

Draw and cut the motor hood as shown in diagram 5. Then draw the two outlines in black on the hood. Also, before attaching the hood, curve it over the edge of your work table or the edge of a ruler. This will bend the paper and make it easier to handle.

Glue the motor hood on in stages. Fold the edge under along line A-B, and glue it so that the fold is at the left edge of the chassis. Then glue the hood over the edges of bulkheads #1 and #2, a section at a time. This has to be done slowly and carefully so the motor hood will fit properly. On the right side, folded line C-D may not end up exactly at the edge of the chassis. Do not become disturbed; this sometimes happens because of the motor hood's slant between bulkheads #1 and #2. Simply make a new fold to match the chassis edge, leaving enough paper to use for gluing tabs. If the gluing tabs are too wide, trim them with your scissors or knife.

Finally, glue the hood and radiator together. Bend the radiator out away from the front edge of the hood. The radiator is flexible so this can be done without difficulty. Put lots of glue along the edge of the radiator, then push it back beneath the hood. Do not push too hard or else the radiator will lean inward. Try to keep it straight.

Motor Hood Trim (Diagram 6)

After the hood is firmly attached, cut a ¼-inch wide strip of white paper (see diagram 6). Make it approximately 4⅜ inches long. Glue the strip to the front edge of the motor hood. After it is firmly attached, it can be trimmed to match the edges of the chassis.

DIAGRAM 5

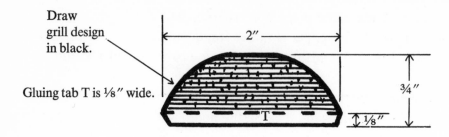

Draw grill design in black.

Gluing tab T is ⅛″ wide.

2″

¾″

⅛″

T

Radiator
Make 1 from white construction paper.

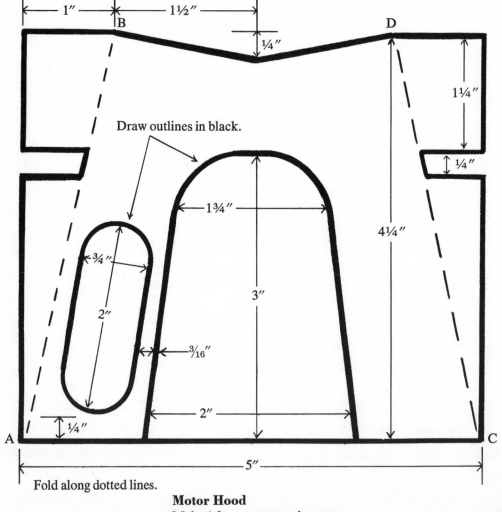

1″

B

1½″

¼″

D

1¼″

¼″

Draw outlines in black.

1¾″

4¼″

¾″

3″

2″

3⁄16″

2″

¼″

A

C

5″

Fold along dotted lines.

Motor Hood
Make 1 from construction paper.

DIAGRAM 6

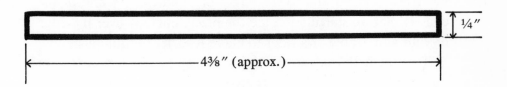

Motor Hood Trim
Make 1 from white paper.

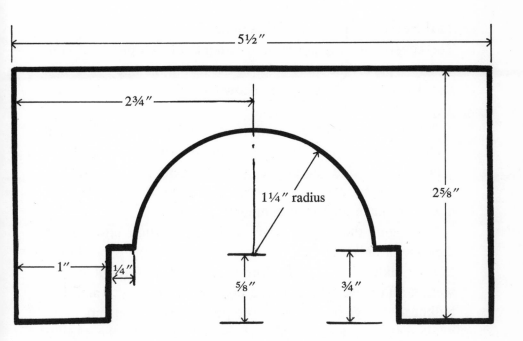

Driver's Compartment Covering
Make 1 from construction paper.

Note: This diagram is not to scale. Draw the covering to the measurements given.

Driver's Compartment Covering (Diagram 6)

The covering for the driver's compartment is made from the same color construction paper as the motor hood. Draw and cut it as shown in diagram 6. The covering is glued to bulkheads #2 and #3 and to the edges of bulkhead #4 and of the chassis. Before starting to glue the piece, curve it over the edge of your work table or a ruler to make it easier to fit in place.

To attach the covering, begin gluing at the top center of bulkheads #2 and #3 and then work down their sides to the edges of the chassis. (The covering will overlap the motor hood by about ⅜ inch.) Again, work slowly, a section at a time, as you glue the covering to the edges of the bulkheads. If there is excess paper left over at the sides, cut it even with the chassis edge with your knife or scissors.

Tail Section Covering (Diagram 7)

The covering of the tail section is made of two pieces of construction paper, the same color as the rest of the body covering. Draw and cut the pieces as shown in diagram 7. Glue one piece at a time.

Begin gluing one tail section at bulkhead #4. The small extension on the piece will extend slightly forward of this bulkhead to the side of the driver's compartment. As you glue the piece along the edge of bulkhead #4, press firmly with your fingers to make a good attachment.

Next, glue the slanted edge of the tail section down along the edge of bulkhead #5. Again, keep pressing the paper firmly to the bulkhead to make a firm attachment. Before gluing the section all the way down to the tail end of the car, attach it to bulkhead #6. Then glue the loose portion to the tail end.

Now glue the loose bottom of the tail section to the edge of the chassis. Start at the tail end and work forward. A bulge in the paper is likely to develop about midway between the tail and the attached end at the driver's seat. Don't panic! Make a

DIAGRAM 7

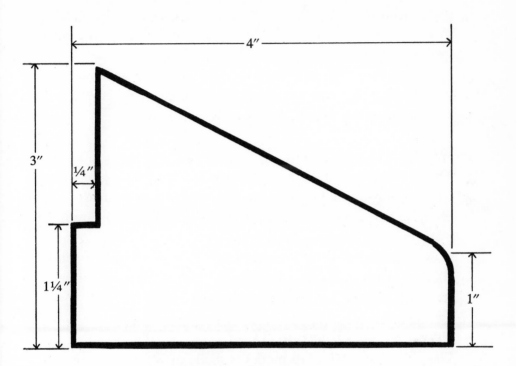

Tail Section Covering
Make 2 from construction paper.

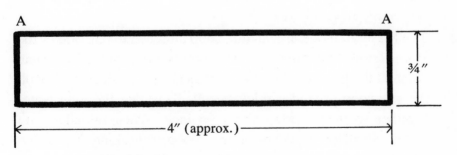

Windshield
Make 1 from white construction paper.

slice in the bulge about 1 inch long with your knife. Glue one side of the sliced paper to the chassis. You may do one of two things with the other sliced portion. You may trim it carefully so that it meets evenly with the other sliced edge, or you may overlap the two edges.

Follow the same procedure for attaching the other tail section. Don't hesitate to use your knife or scissors to remove any excess paper for nice clean edges.

Windshield (Diagram 7)

The windshield of the Maserati model is simply a strip of white construction paper glued inside the upper curved edge of the driver's compartment. Draw and cut it as shown in diagram 7. Corners A-A of the windshield are glued even with the corners at the sides of the driver's compartment. The windshield extends about ½ inch above the curved edge of the driver's compartment when glued. See the photo on page 138.

Driver's Seat (Diagram 8)

The seat of the Maserati model is made of black construction paper. Draw and cut it as shown in diagram 8, measuring it carefully. Fold the seat as in the diagram and glue it inside the driver's compartment, using gluing tabs T to attach it.

Air Scoop (Diagram 9)

The Maserati model has an air scoop attached to one side of the motor hood. Make this part with construction paper, the same color as the hood. Draw and cut it as shown in diagram 9. Roll the air scoop around a thick pencil, then glue the long edges together so they overlap about ⅜ inch. When the edges are firmly glued, press down on the scoop, squashing it slightly. This will give the scoop an oval shape, about ⅝ inch across its widest opening.

Glue the scoop, wide end pointing forward, to the right side

DIAGRAM 8

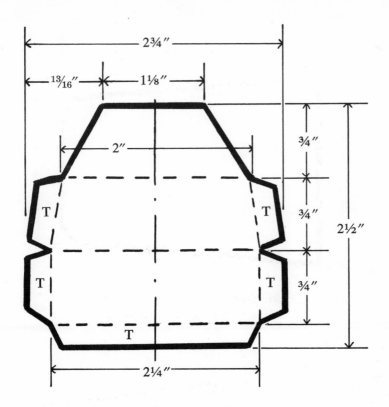

Driver's Seat
Make 1 from black construction paper.
Gluing tabs T are ¼″ wide.

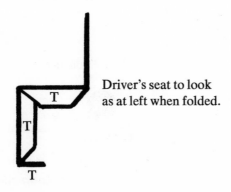

Driver's seat to look
as at left when folded.

DIAGRAM 9

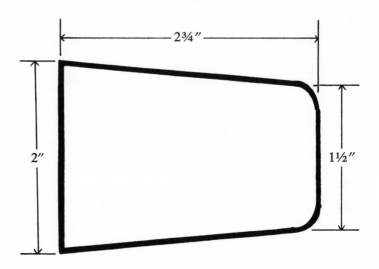

Air Scoop
Make 1 from construction paper.

Speedometer
Make 1 from black
construction paper.

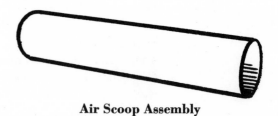

Air Scoop Assembly

Oil Gauge
¼″ diameter

Fuel Gauge
⅜″ diameter

Make 1 of each from
black construction paper.

of the motor hood. See the photo on page 148 for the scoop's correct position. Make certain that you glue the seam of the scoop against the hood so it will not show on the finished model.

Gauges (Diagram 9)

Three gauges are installed on the Maserati model—a speedometer, an oil gauge, and a fuel gauge. Draw and cut all three from black construction paper as shown in diagram 9. The gauges are glued to the dashboard (bulkhead #3) facing the driver. Tweezers will be helpful for handling these small pieces. See diagram 10 for correct placement of the gauges.

Gas and Brake Pedals (Diagram 10)

The gas and brake pedals are made of rigid cardboard. Draw and cut them as shown in diagram 10. The pedals are painted black with India ink or poster paint. They are simply glued at an angle at the bottom of the dashboard: one end of each pedal is glued to the dashboard, the other end to the chassis floor. See diagram 10 for their correct positions.

DIAGRAM 10

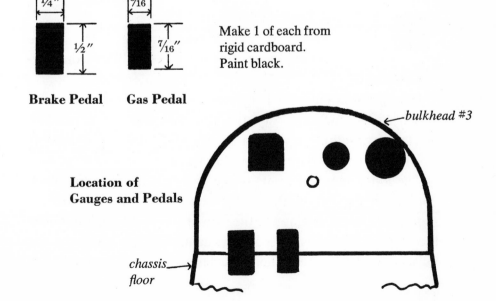

Make 1 of each from rigid cardboard. Paint black.

Brake Pedal   Gas Pedal

Location of Gauges and Pedals

bulkhead #3

chassis floor

Engine Exhaust Unit (Diagram 11)

The engine exhaust unit is made of two drinking straws. These are wrapped in and held together by a piece of black construction paper.

One straw is cut to a length of 6½ inches, the other to a length of 5½ inches. Wrap and glue the straws in a piece of black construction paper 3½ inches long and approximately 1⅛ inches wide. Overlap and glue the edges.

The long, uncovered part of the straws is glued to the black outline on the left of the motor hood. The covered portion, slightly flattened, is glued to the side of the body, slightly below the edge of the driver's compartment. See the photo of the finished model to check the placement.

DIAGRAM 11

Engine Exhaust Unit

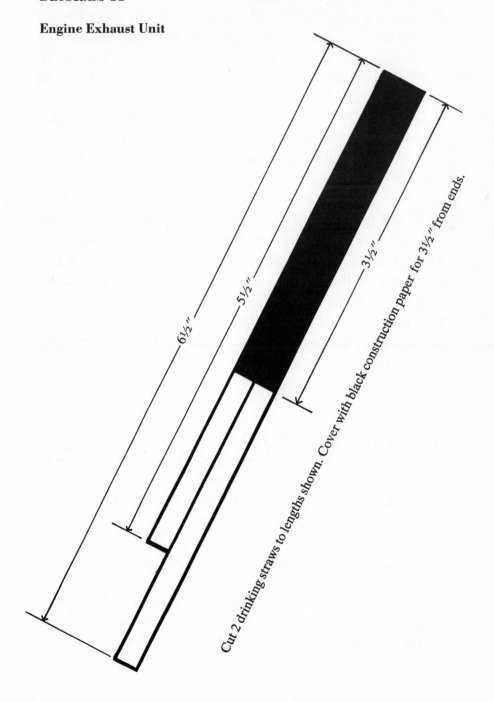

6½"

5½"

3½"

Cut 2 drinking straws to lengths shown. Cover with black construction paper for 3½" from ends.

Steering Wheel (Diagram 12)

The steering wheel of the Maserati model has two parts—a steering column and the wheel itself. The steering column is a 2-inch length of a large wooden matchstick. Both ends of the steering column are cut at an angle (see diagram 12). Paint the steering column black with India ink or poster paint.

The steering wheel is simply a disc, 1¼ inches in diameter, cut from rigid cardboard. Draw the wheel design—rim and spokes—with India ink as shown in diagram 12. Glue the wheel to one end of the column. Put lots of glue in the center of the wheel; then place the column exactly in the center of the wheel and hold it there for a few moments until the glue sets.

After the steering wheel and column are firmly joined, install the steering wheel in the model. Put a generous amount of glue on the end of the column and push it through the hole in the dashboard. When you feel the column end touch the chassis floor behind the dashboard, hold it for a few moments until the glue sets. Put some glue at the point where the column goes through the dashboard hole to make the part doubly secure.

Hand Brake (Diagram 12)

The hand brake has two parts—a shaft made from a round toothpick and a triangular base made from rigid cardboard. Cut the shaft to 1⅛ inches as shown in diagram 12 and paint it yellow with poster paint.

Cut the triangular base as shown in diagram 12. Paint it black with India ink or poster paint. Then glue the shaft to the base as shown in diagram 12.

Glue the hand brake unit to the floor of the driver's compartment against the bottom edge of the dashboard; locate it a short distance to the left of the brake pedal (the one closer to the left side).

DIAGRAM 12

2″

Cut ends
at an angle.

Steering Column
Make 1 from large matchstick.
Paint black.

1¼″ diameter

Steering Wheel
Make 1 from
rigid cardboard.
Draw design in black.

**Steering Wheel
Assembly**

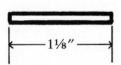

1⅛″

Hand Brake Shaft
Make 1 from
round toothpick.
Paint yellow.

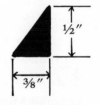

½″

⅜″

Hand Brake Base
Make 1 from
rigid cardboard.
Paint black.

Hand Brake Assembly

Gear Shift (Diagram 13)

The gear shift unit is made up of three parts—a base, a shaft, and a hand grip. The base is drawn and cut from construction paper as shown in diagram 13. Follow the measurements carefully; make the hole and draw the design in black as shown.

The shaft is a 1-inch length of round toothpick. The hand grip is a ⅜-inch length cut from a wooden matchstick. Cut both ends of the grip at an angle (see diagram 13). Paint the grip and the shaft black. Then glue the grip to one end of the shaft to form a T-shaped piece as shown in the diagram.

Fold the base on the dotted lines and glue the shaft in the hole; diagram 13 shows how the completed unit should look. Then glue the assembled gear shift unit to the floor of the driver's compartment on the right side. Place it a short distance in from the side of the compartment.

Fuel Tank Cap (Diagram 14)

The fuel tank cap is made of two discs cut from rigid cardboard. Disc A is ⅜ inch in diameter; disc B is ¼ inch in diameter. Glue the larger disc A to disc B, and paint the assembled cap with aluminum paint.

Glue the fuel tank cap to the top of bulkhead #4, directly behind the driver's seat. See the photos of the finished model for placement (pages 128, 138, and 148).

Rear View Mirror (Diagram 14)

The rear view mirror has two parts made from rigid cardboard —a bracket and a mirror. Draw and cut the pieces as shown in diagram 14. The mirror is simply a disc ⅜ inch in diameter; paint one side black and the other side with aluminum paint. Paint the bracket black.

Glue the black side of the mirror to one end of the bracket as shown in diagram 14. The mirror unit is then glued on the left side of the driver's compartment, at the point where the

DIAGRAM 13

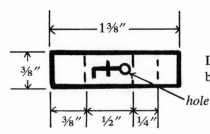

Draw design in black and make hole before folding along dotted lines.

Gear Shift Base
Make 1 from
construction paper.

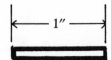

Gear Shift Shaft
Make 1 from
round toothpick.
Paint black.

Gear Shift Hand Grip
Make 1 from
large matchstick.
Paint black.

Shaft and Hand Grip Assembly

Gear Shift Assembly

DIAGRAM 14

Fuel Tank Cap

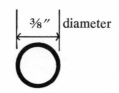

⅜″ diameter

Disc A
Make 1 from
rigid cardboard.

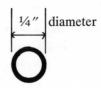

¼″ diameter

Disc B
Make 1 from
rigid cardboard.

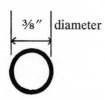

⅜″ diameter

Rear View Mirror
Make 1 from
rigid cardboard.

A

B

**Fuel Tank
Cap Assembly**

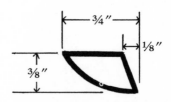

¾″

⅛″

⅜″

Bracket
Make 1 from
rigid cardboard.

**Rear View Mirror
Assembly**

windshield slants into the body of the driver's section. Put glue along the long straight edge of the bracket and hold it in place on the model for a few moments while the glue sets. See the photo on page 138 for correct placement.

Wheels and Axles (Diagram 15)

The four wheels of the Maserati model are cut from rigid cardboard. They are 2 inches in diameter. Draw the design on each side of each wheel as shown in diagram 15. Use India ink or black poster paint to fill in the tire. Pen and ink are best for drawing the spokes.

The two axles are 3¼-inch lengths of large wooden matchsticks. Paint them black with India ink or poster paint.

DIAGRAM 15

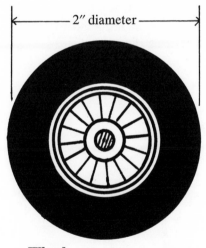

2″ diameter

Draw design in black;
draw hubcap in same color
as car body.

Wheel
Make 4 from rigid cardboard.

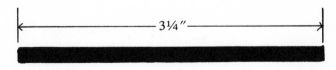

Make 2 from
large matchsticks.
Paint black.

3¼″

Axle

DIAGRAM 16

Wheel Brake Strip
Make 8 from
rigid cardboard.
Paint black.

¾″ diameter

Make hole
in center
for axle end.

Wheel Brake Disc
Make 4 from
rigid cardboard.
Paint black.

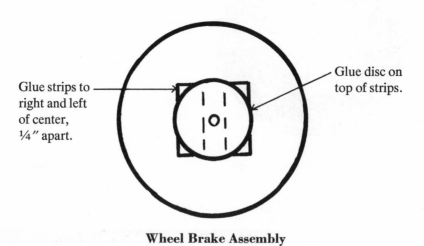

Glue strips to
right and left
of center,
¼″ apart.

Glue disc on
top of strips.

Wheel Brake Assembly

Wheel Brakes (Diagram 16)

Four wheel brakes are needed for joining the wheels to the axles. Each brake consists of two short strips of rigid cardboard and a disc also of rigid cardboard. See diagram 16 for the sizes and shapes of these pieces. Paint the pieces black.

Two strips are glued on one side of each wheel; this will become the inner or axle side of the wheel. Place and glue the strips about ¼ inch apart, on each side of the center of each wheel. With a nail or other sharp pointed tool, punch a hole in the center of each disc; make the holes large enough for the ends of the axles to fit through. Then glue one disc on top of each pair of strips, forming a kind of bridge (see diagram 16).

Wheel and Axle Assembly

After the wheel brakes are securely in place, glue the wheels, one at a time, to the ends of the axles. Lay a wheel flat on the table and put a generous amount of glue in the hole of the disc. Push one end of an axle through the hole and hold it firmly for a few moments until the glue sets. Be sure to keep the axle as straight as you possibly can. If the wheels are crooked, your model will not rest evenly on its wheels.

When the four wheels have been firmly attached to the axles, glue each set of wheels to the underside of the racer. The front pair is attached 1¾ inches from the front end. The rear pair is mounted 2¾ inches from the tail end of the body.

Again, make certain that the two sets of wheels are perfectly straight in relation to the racer's body and that each wheel is the same distance out from the sides of the body. Check this by looking straight down at your model from above.

Wheel Fins (Diagram 17)

Two wheel fins, one on each side, are attached to the Maserati racer. The fins are drawn and cut from rigid cardboard as shown in diagram 17. Paint the fins with poster paint the same color as the racer's body.

Each fin is glued to the lower edge of the body about ⅛ inch behind the front wheels. The long straight side (the 1-inch length) is glued to the body. The ½-inch straight side is at the front. Hold each fin in place until the glue sets, keeping it as straight as possible in relation to the body. Do not let the fins tilt downward. See the photo of the finished model for placement.

Number (Diagram 17)

The Maserati model carries the number 1 in two places. Draw and cut two numbers from white paper as shown in diagram 17.

Glue one number on the right side of the motor hood at the front. Attach it at a slight angle in relation to the front end. Glue the second number on the tail end of the body on the left side. See the photo on page 138 for placement of the rear number.

Vents (Diagram 17)

The addition of fifteen small vents will complete the Maserati model. The vents are shaped as half-moons. Cut them from black construction paper as shown in diagram 17.

The vents are glued to the model in groups of three. Two groups of three vents each are glued to the top of the motor hood toward the driver's compartment. Two more groups of three vents each are glued to the left and right sides of the body in front of the driver's compartment. All these vents are glued with their straight edges facing forward.

The last group of vents is glued to the tail end of the body with their straight edges facing the number. See the photo on page 128 for placement of the tail vents.

Because the vents are so small, use tweezers for holding and gluing them. Try to attach the vents in as straight a line and as equally spaced as possible.

Attaching the vents will give the final touch to your Maserati racer. You should feel great satisfaction at the surprisingly close resemblance between the finished model and the real Maserati.

DIAGRAM 17

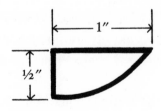

Wheel Fin
Make 2 from rigid cardboard.
Paint same color as car body.

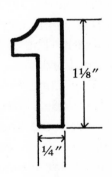

Number
Make 2 from
white paper.

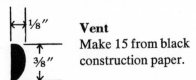

Vent
Make 15 from black
construction paper.

Lotus-Ford: 1963

In the great Lotus-Ford Formula 1 racer of the 1960s, the driver lay almost flat on his back as he guided the vehicle. INDIANAPOLIS MOTOR SPEEDWAY OFFICIAL PHOTO

The Ford Motor Company entered Grand Prix racing competition in the early 1960s. At that time Ford engineers combined their technical skills with the superlative talents of an English designer of racing cars, Colin Chapman. The engineers redesigned a standard Ford engine for racing, mainly for more power, while Chapman produced a sleek, streamlined body to house it. The result of this international team effort was the Lotus-Ford.

Two Lotus-Fords were built for the Indianapolis 500 race in May 1963. A buzz of excitement ran through the spectators when they saw the unusual-looking racers. The cars were radically different from most of the other competitors in that their engines were mounted in the rear. The Lotus-Fords were also different in size—almost midgets by comparison with the other racers.

150

The body of the Lotus-Ford was built close to the ground to better hug the roadway at high speed. The car was exceptionally maneuverable, particularly on curves. It was often described as a vehicle tailored around the driver, who lay almost flat on his back while guiding the auto at blistering speeds of nearly 200 miles per hour.

Although the Lotus-Fords were not winners in the 1963 Indy 500, they achieved a long string of victories in later years, in both the United States and Europe. More significantly, they established new standards for racing cars, especially for Grand Prix competition. After 1963, rear-mounted engines in racing cars became extremely popular. Among other advantages of this new feature was a great reduction in weight, since cumbersome driveshafts could be eliminated. The rear engine also made better streamlining possible for reduced air resistance.

The model you will build is the revolutionary Lotus-Ford of 1963.

BUILDING THE LOTUS-FORD MODEL

Chassis (Diagram 1)
The chassis is made of rigid cardboard. Draw and cut it as shown in diagram 1.

Bulkheads (Diagram 2)
As in some of the other models in this book, bulkheads are used in the Lotus-Ford model to form a sturdy body. Four bulkheads are needed. Make them from rigid cardboard. Draw and cut the bulkheads as shown in diagram 2.

After cutting out the bulkheads as carefully as you can, glue them to the chassis in an upright position. See diagram 3 for their location. When gluing, be sure to hold the bulkheads as straight as possible. If any of them are crooked, it will be difficult to glue the body covering properly.

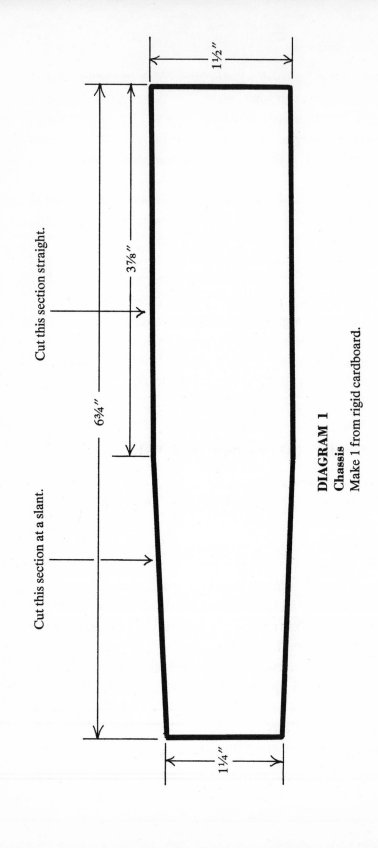

DIAGRAM 1
Chassis
Make 1 from rigid cardboard.

Cut this section straight.

Cut this section at a slant.

1½"

3⅞"

6¾"

1¼"

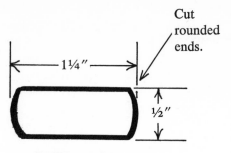

Cut rounded ends.

$1\frac{1}{4}''$

$\frac{1}{2}''$

Bulkhead #1
Make 1 from
rigid cardboard.

DIAGRAM 2

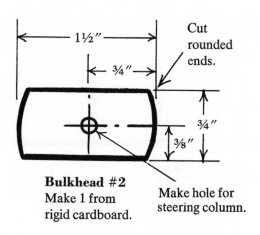

$1\frac{1}{2}''$

$\frac{3}{4}''$

Cut rounded ends.

$\frac{3}{4}''$

$\frac{3}{8}''$

Bulkhead #2
Make 1 from
rigid cardboard.

Make hole for
steering column.

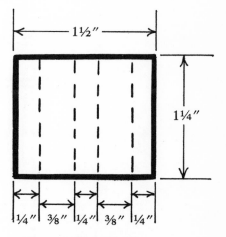

$1\frac{1}{2}''$

$1\frac{1}{4}''$

$\frac{1}{4}''$ $\frac{3}{8}''$ $\frac{1}{4}''$ $\frac{3}{8}''$ $\frac{1}{4}''$

Front Wheel Mount
Make 1 this size
from construction paper.

Rear wheel mount
is made the same way,
except that it is
$\frac{7}{8}''$ long instead of $1\frac{1}{4}''$.

Fold on dotted lines.

Glue wheel mounts to form
a hollow box shape as above.

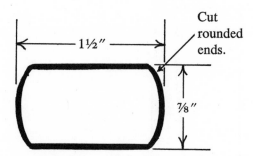

Cut rounded ends.

$1\frac{1}{2}''$

$\frac{7}{8}''$

Bulkheads #3 and #4
Make 2 from
rigid cardboard.

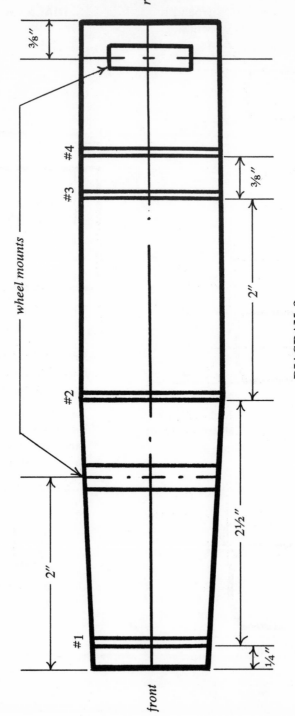

DIAGRAM 3

**Location of Bulkheads
and Wheel Mounts**

Wheel Mounts (Diagram 2)

Two wheel mounts are needed for attaching the axles and wheels to the model. The mounts are rectangular box-like units made of construction paper. Use any color paper you wish.

Draw and cut the front wheel mount as shown in diagram 2. Then draw and cut the rear wheel mount; it is like the front one, except that it is ⅞ inch long instead of 1¼ inches.

The mounts are glued to the top of the chassis. See diagram 3 for their location. Be careful when attaching the mounts to keep them parallel to the front and rear edges of the chassis. If the mounts are crooked, the wheels of the model will also be crooked.

Nose Covering (Diagram 4)

The nose covering of the Lotus-Ford is made of green construction paper, or any other color you wish. Draw and cut the nose covering as shown in diagram 4.

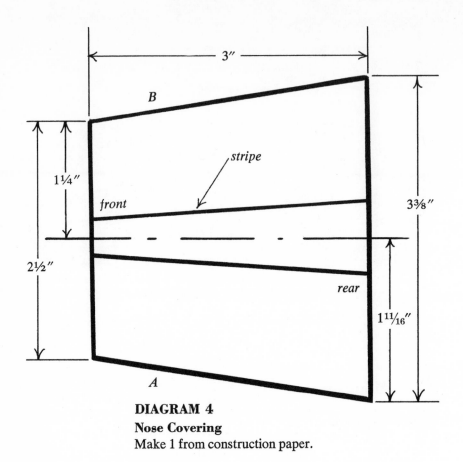

DIAGRAM 4
Nose Covering
Make 1 from construction paper.

To attach the nose covering, first check to see that it fits the front section properly. You may have to trim the piece here and there, and curve it by sliding it over the edge of your work table or the edge of a ruler. Start attaching the nose covering by putting glue along either edge A or edge B. Whichever one you begin with, make sure that it is even with the edge of the chassis. When this edge is firmly glued, start attaching the covering over the edges of bulkheads #1 and #2. Glue one short section of the covering at a time. Rub each glued portion several times with your finger to make sure the covering sticks to the edges of the bulkheads. You will end by gluing the second edge of the nose covering to the opposite edge of the chassis.

156

DIAGRAM 5

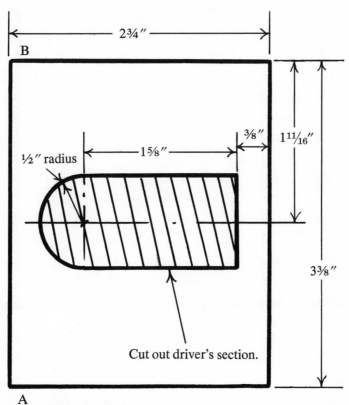

B

2¾″

½″ radius

1⅝″

⅜″

1¹¹⁄₁₆″

3⅜″

Cut out driver's section.

A

Body Covering
Make 1 from construction paper.

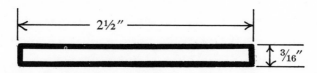

2½″

³⁄₁₆″

Front Nose Stripe
Make 1 from construction paper.

Body Covering (Diagram 5)

The covering for the body section is made from the same color construction paper as the nose covering. It is a rectangular piece with a cut-out section for the driver's compartment. Draw and cut the body covering as shown in diagram 5.

Follow the same procedure for attaching the body covering as you did for gluing the nose covering. First try the piece to see that it fits properly. Since the covering will be curved, it will make gluing easier if the paper is first curved over the edge of your work table or a ruler.

Start gluing, using either edge A or edge B of the body covering. Again, make certain that the edge is even with the edge of the chassis. When this edge is firmly glued, attach one portion of the covering at a time to the edges of bulkheads #2, #3, and #4. You will end by gluing the free edge of the covering to the opposite edge of the chassis. If there is excess paper at the edge, trim it with your scissors or knife.

Trim (Diagrams 5-6)

The model of the Lotus-Ford racer has stripes on the front edge and the center of the nose covering and three discs with racing numbers. The stripes and discs are made from yellow construction paper. The numbers are made from black construction paper.

The front nose stripe is simply a strip $\frac{3}{16}$ inch wide and $2\frac{1}{2}$ inches long (see diagram 5). It is glued around the front edge of the nose covering. Be sure to keep it even with the edge of the nose covering while gluing.

The center nose stripe is a tapered piece. Draw and cut it as shown in diagram 6. The broad end of the tapered stripe is glued at the driver's end of the nose section. The narrow end is glued to the front edge. When gluing this stripe, be certain it is exactly along the center of the nose.

The three discs are $\frac{3}{4}$ inch in diameter (see diagram 6).

DIAGRAM 6

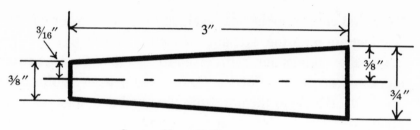

Center Nose Stripe
Make 1 from construction paper.

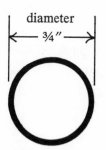

Disc
Make 3 from
construction paper.

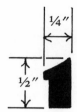

Number
Make 3 from black
construction paper.

Number Disc
Assembly

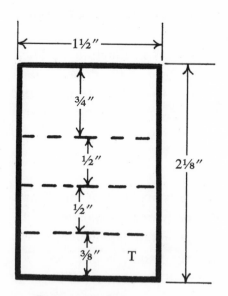

Driver's Seat
Make 1 from black
construction paper.

Glue to
bulkhead →
#3.

Glue tab T
to chassis floor.

Driver's seat to look
as above when folded.

Draw and cut a number 1 to be glued to the center of each disc. See diagram 6 for the style and size of the numbers.

One disc with its number is glued to the top of the nose covering, close to the edge of the driver's compartment. Place the disc in the middle of the nose with the number at an angle. The other two discs are glued to the right and left sides of the racer's body at the driver's compartment. Attach them with the numbers straight up and down. See the photo of the finished model for placement (page 164).

Driver's Seat (Diagram 6)
The driver's seat is made from black construction paper. Draw and cut the seat as shown in diagram 6. Before gluing the seat in place, make sure that it fits properly. You may have to trim it here and there before you are satisfied.

Hand Brake (Diagram 7)
The hand brake of the Lotus-Ford model has two parts—a length of round toothpick for the handle and a triangle of rigid cardboard for the base. See diagram 7 for the sizes and shapes of these pieces. Paint both pieces black with India ink or poster paint.

Glue the handle to the base as shown in diagram 7. Then glue the assembled hand brake to the floor of the driver's compartment. Attach it on the left, about ¼ inch in front of the driver's seat and the same distance from the left side of the compartment.

Gear Shift (Diagram 7)
The gear shift of the Grand Prix racer is made up of three parts —a length of round toothpick for the handle, a shorter length of round toothpick for a knob at one end of the handle, and a two-layer cardboard base to which the handle is attached. See diagram 7 for the sizes and shapes of all the pieces. All parts of

160

DIAGRAM 7

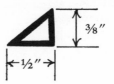

Hand Brake Handle
Make 1 from
round toothpick.
Paint black.

Hand Brake Base
Make 1 from
rigid cardboard.
Paint black.

**Hand Brake
Assembly**

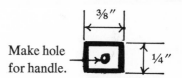

Gear Shift Knob
Make 1 from
round toothpick.
Paint black.

Gear Shift Handle
Make 1 from
round toothpick.
Paint black.

Gear Shift Base
Make 2 from
rigid cardboard.
Paint black.
Glue pieces together
for double thickness.

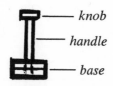

knob

handle

base

Gear Shift Assembly

the gear shift are painted black with India ink or poster paint.

Glue the gear shift together as shown in diagram 7. The assembled gear shift is glued to the floor of the driver's compartment on the right. Locate it about ¼ inch in front of the driver's seat and about the same distance from the right side of the compartment.

Brake and Gas Pedals (Diagram 8)

The brake and gas pedals are both made from rigid cardboard. Draw and cut them as shown in diagram 8. Paint both pedals black with India ink or poster paint.

The brake pedal is glued at a slant with one end resting against the lower part of bulkhead #2 (the dashboard) and the other end glued to the floor. Locate the brake pedal about ¼ inch from the left side of the driver's compartment.

The gas pedal is glued the same way, ¼ inch to the right of the brake pedal. See diagram 8 for placement of the pedals.

Speedometer (Diagram 8)

The speedometer is simply a disc of black construction paper, ⅜ inch in diameter (see diagram 8). It is glued on the right side of the dashboard, as shown in diagram 8.

You may wish to add more instruments to the dashboard of your Lotus-Ford model. Make them from black construction paper in various shapes and sizes, and glue them on the dashboard. For holding these small pieces while gluing, tweezers will be helpful.

Steering Wheel (Diagram 8)

The steering wheel unit consists of a steering column and a steering wheel. The steering column is a 1⅜-inch length of a large wooden matchstick with the ends cut at an angle. The wheel is made from rigid cardboard; see diagram 8 for its size and design. Paint the steering column red and draw the design on the wheel in red too.

162

DIAGRAM 8

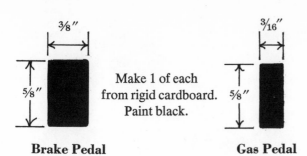

Make 1 of each from rigid cardboard. Paint black.

Brake Pedal

Gas Pedal

diameter
3/8"

Speedometer
Make 1 from black construction paper.

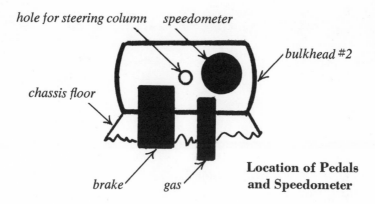

hole for steering column   speedometer

bulkhead #2

chassis floor

brake   gas

Location of Pedals and Speedometer

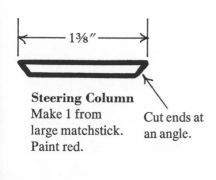

Steering Column
Make 1 from large matchstick. Paint red.

Cut ends at an angle.

diameter
7/8"

Steering Wheel
Make 1 from rigid cardboard.

Draw design on both sides in red.

Steering Wheel Assembly

Glue the wheel to one end of the steering column. When the two pieces are firmly joined, attach the whole unit to the model. Put a generous amount of glue on the free end of the steering column and push it through the hole in the dashboard. When you feel the column end touch the chassis floor behind the dashboard, hold it for a few moments until the glue sets. Finally, put some glue at the point where the column enters the hole in the dashboard to strengthen the steering unit.

Windshield (Diagram 9)

The windshield is made of white construction paper. Draw and cut it as shown in diagram 9. Since the windshield is glued in a curved position, it will help to first curve it over the edge of your work table or your ruler. Glue the windshield around the front edge of the driver's compartment. It will be necessary to hold it in place one section at a time until it is firmly attached. See the photo of the finished model for placement.

164

Rear View Mirrors (Diagram 9)

Two rear view mirrors are needed for the Lotus-Ford model. One is attached to the right side and one to the left side of the driver's compartment. The two mirrors are made exactly alike. Draw and cut the two pieces for each mirror as shown in diagram 9. Use rigid cardboard for the brackets and construction paper for the mirrors themselves. The brackets and mirrors are painted with aluminum paint.

Glue one mirror disc to the ¼-inch edge of each bracket. See diagram 9 for the mirror assembly. Then glue one rear view mirror on each side of the driver's compartment; place the pointed ends of the brackets about even with the pointed ends of the windshield, and they will be positioned correctly.

Safety Roll Bar (Diagram 9)

The Lotus-Ford racer was equipped with a roll bar to protect the driver from being crushed in case of a roll-over accident. For the model, this safety feature is made from two 2-inch lengths of pipe cleaner. See diagram 9 for the shape to bend them. After bending, paint them with aluminum paint. Then glue the two arches together at the top, as shown in diagram 10.

To install the safety roll bar, punch two holes ¾ inch apart, directly behind the driver's compartment. Put glue on the ends of one bar and push them into the holes; be careful not to push them in too far. The other pair of ends is glued to the top rear edge of the body, which is the top edge of bulkhead #4. Hold these ends in place for a few moments until the glue sets. See the photo of the finished model for placement of the roll bar.

Wheels (Diagram 10)

The wheels of the Lotus-Ford racer are big and chunky with extremely broad tires. Each wheel is made up of three main parts—the wheel cylinder, two wheel covers, and two wheel blocks.

DIAGRAM 9

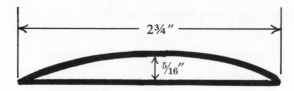

2¾″

⁵⁄₁₆″

Windshield
Make 1 from white construction paper.

diameter
⅜″

⅜″

¼″

Rear View Mirror
Make 2 from
construction paper.
Paint both sides
with aluminum
paint.

Rear View Mirror Bracket
Make 2 from
rigid cardboard.
Paint with
aluminum paint.

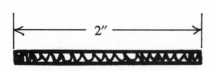

bracket →   ← mirror

Rear View Mirror Assembly

2″

Safety Roll Bar
Make 2 from pipe cleaner.
Paint with aluminum paint.

⅞″

Bend each bar to this shape.

DIAGRAM 10

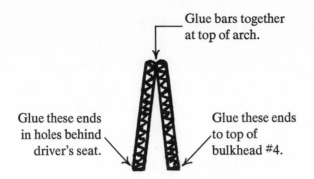

Glue bars together
at top of arch.

Glue these ends
in holes behind
driver's seat.

Glue these ends
to top of
bulkhead #4.

Safety Roll Bar Assembly

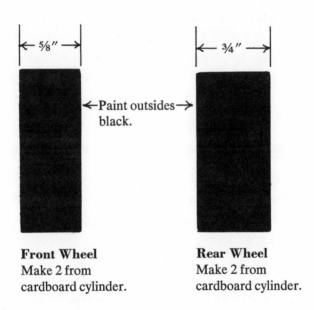

←— ⅝″ —→

←— ¾″ —→

←Paint outsides→
black.

Front Wheel
Make 2 from
cardboard cylinder.

Rear Wheel
Make 2 from
cardboard cylinder.

Make each wheel cylinder from a section of a cardboard cylinder from a roll of paper toweling. (If you have difficulty finding that size cylinder, one from a roll of toilet tissue can be substituted.) Cut two sections from the cylinder ⅝ inch wide, and two sections ¾ inch wide (see diagram 10). The narrower pair will become the front wheels, the wider pair the rear wheels. Paint the outside of each wheel black.

Wheel Covers (Diagram 11)

To close the wheel cylinders, cut eight discs, approximately 1%16 inches in diameter, from white construction paper. These discs form the outer and inner covers for the wheels. Draw the design of concentric circles in black on one side of each wheel cover, as shown in diagram 11.

Wheel Blocks (Diagram 11)

On the plain sides of four of the wheel covers, glue two small pieces of rigid cardboard measuring ⅜ inch wide and ½ inch long. These are the wheel blocks (see diagram 11). Glue the pieces on each side of the center of the wheel cover, parallel to one another and with just enough space between them for the end of the axle to fit properly. The wheel blocks will support the ends of the axles when these are joined to the wheels. Glue the wheel blocks only to the four covers that will be on the outer sides of the wheels.

Wheel Assembly

After the wheel blocks have been glued, attach all the wheel covers to the wheel cylinders. Lay each cover flat on your work surface. Then place a generous amount of glue around the rim of the cylinder and press it down against the cover. Make sure you attach one disc with wheel blocks and one without them to each cylinder, and keep the sides with the drawn designs facing out. Match the discs to the openings of the cylinders as closely as possible. If there is any overhang, trim it carefully with your scissors or knife. When all the discs have been glued, place your ruler across the wheels and a medium weight, such as a bottle of ink, on top of the ruler. This will help attach the covers to the cylinders firmly.

As you can see in the photos of the finished model, all four wheels are painted black with India ink or poster paint. However, do not paint the entire wheel cover—just paint the outer circle that represents the tire.

DIAGRAM 11

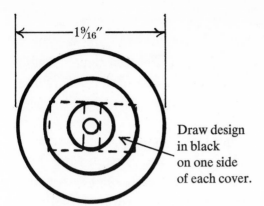

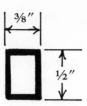

Draw design
in black
on one side
of each cover.

Wheel Block
Make 8 from
rigid cardboard.

Glue two wheel
blocks to inside
of each outer wheel
cover at center.

Wheel Cover
Make 8 from white
construction paper.

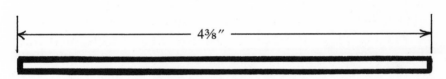

Axle
Make 2 from large matchsticks.
Paint black.

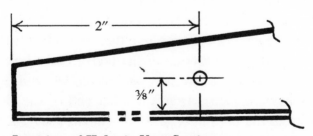

Location of Holes in Nose Section
Make hole on each side of nose section for front axle.

Axles (Diagram 11)

The axles for the Lotus-Ford racer are 4⅜-inch lengths of large matchsticks (see diagram 11). The axles are painted black with India ink or poster paint.

Wheel and Axle Assembly

Start joining the wheels to the axles by gluing one front wheel to an end of one axle. Make a hole in the center of the inside wheel cover (the one without the wheel blocks). Use a nail or the point of your scissors to start the hole and enlarge it just enough so the matchstick can slide through easily.

Try the axle through the hole before gluing. Feel for the two wheel blocks on the inside of the outer wheel cover that will support the end of the axle. You can't see these pieces, of course, since they are now inside the covered wheel, so you will have to keep trying until you succeed in sliding the axle end between them. This is not really as difficult as it sounds.

Once you are sure of finding the two wheel blocks, withdraw the axle, put a generous blob of glue on its end, and push it back through the hole. Again, make sure you can feel it fit between the two wheel blocks inside the wheel. Check with your eye to see that the wheel is on the axle straight. Once you are satisfied about this, turn the wheel onto its outer cover with the axle pointing straight up. Put some glue around the point where the axle enters the inner wheel cover; this will help join the wheel and axle more securely.

Now that you have one front wheel attached to the axle, the next step is to glue this assembly to the model. Begin by making two holes in the nose section of the body. These holes are perfectly in line with one another, one on the left and one on the right. Measure 2 inches from the front end of the chassis and ⅜ inch from the bottom edge of the chassis (see diagram 11). These measurements will place the holes slightly above the front wheel mount.

Try sliding the axle through the holes before doing any gluing. Put the second front wheel on the end of the axle temporarily and check to make sure everything fits properly. Be sure you use the other ⅝-inch front wheel, not a ¾-inch rear wheel.

When you are satisfied with the way the wheel and axle fit, glue them in place. Put a generous amount of glue on the end of the axle and also along its length, which will rest on the front wheel mount. Push the axle through the holes and attach the wheel, making sure it is on straight. Also be careful to keep both front wheels the same distance out from the racer's sides. Rest the front end of the model on a support until the wheel and axle assembly is firmly attached.

The rear wheels are easier to attach since the rear portion of the racer has no body covering and the rear wheel mount is exposed. Glue both rear wheels to the ends of the axle, making certain they are straight. When they are tightly joined to the axle, glue the whole assembly to the wheel mount. Put lots of glue along the top of the wheel mount, place the axle on it, and press firmly. Make sure the wheels are the same distance out from the racer's sides and in line with the front wheels.

Rest the rear portion of the racer on a support until the glue hardens.

Axle Supports (Diagram 12)

While the wheel and axle assembly is drying, cut four axle supports. These are ⅞-inch lengths cut from round toothpicks (see diagram 12). The supports are painted black with India ink or poster paint.

Glue each axle support to the racer at an angle, with one end on the body of the model and the other end on the axle. See diagram 12 and the overhead photo of the finished model on page 176 for their placement.

DIAGRAM 12

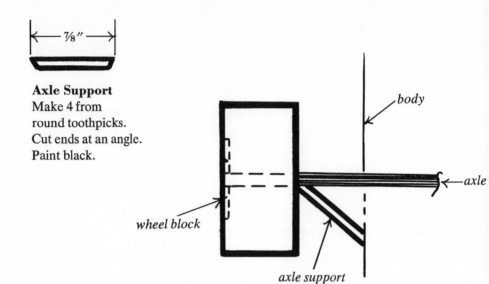

Axle Support
Make 4 from
round toothpicks.
Cut ends at an angle.
Paint black.

**Overhead View of
Axle Support Assembly**

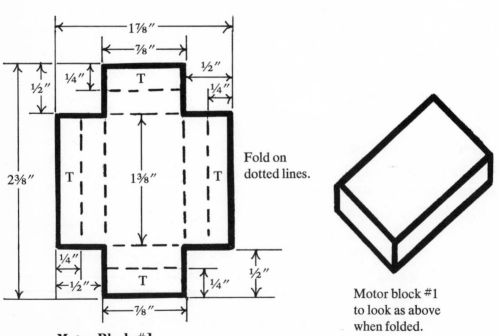

Fold on
dotted lines.

Motor Block #1
Make 1 from construction paper.

Motor block #1
to look as above
when folded.

Engine (Diagrams 12-14)

The main part of the racer's engine consists of two box-like units, block #1 and block #2. The blocks are made of different-colored construction paper. Draw and cut the blocks as shown in diagrams 12 and 13.

Eight air vents are also needed for the engine. These are ⅜-inch lengths of a drinking straw (see diagram 14). Paint each vent with aluminum paint. Then glue them upright in a double row on the top side of block #1; see diagram 14 for their placement.

When the vents are attached, glue the motor blocks to the rear of the chassis, directly behind the driver's compartment. Begin by gluing motor block #2 (the thicker one) in position between the rear wheel mount and bulkhead #4 (the back of the driver's compartment). The block is fitted lengthwise across the chassis.

Next, glue block #1 (the one with the air vents) on top of and at right angles to block #2. It extends lengthwise from the back of bulkhead #4 across the rear axle to the rear end of the model. See diagram 14 and the photo of the finished model.

Tail Pipes (Diagram 14)

The engine of the Lotus-Ford racer has two tail pipes. These are made from 2-inch lengths of large-size drinking straws (see diagram 14). The two pipes are painted with aluminum paint.

Each pipe has a small triangular support to hold it in an upward slanted position. The supports are made from rigid cardboard; draw and cut them as shown in diagram 14. Paint each support black with India ink or poster paint.

Glue each support on its edge at the tail end of the chassis, ⅛ inch in from each side. The bottom point of the support, on the slanted side, should almost touch motor block #2.

After the supports are firmly glued, attach the tail pipes. These are positioned along the slanted sides of the supports.

DIAGRAM 13

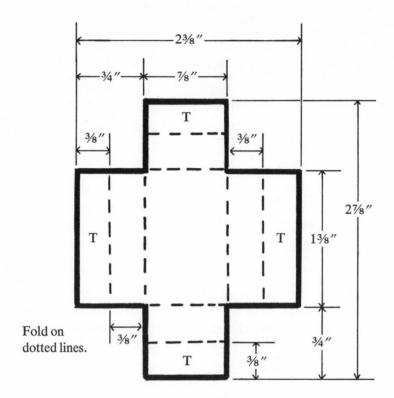

2⅜″

¾″ ⅞″

T

⅜″ ⅜″

2⅞″

T T 1⅜″

Fold on
dotted lines.

⅜″

T ¾″

⅜″

Motor Block #2
Make 1 from construction paper.

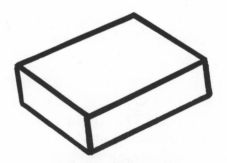

Motor block #2 to look
as above when folded.

DIAGRAM 14

Air Vent
Make 8 from large
drinking straw.
Paint with aluminum paint.

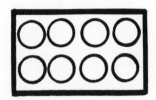

Location of Air Vents
Glue vents upright
on top of motor block #1.

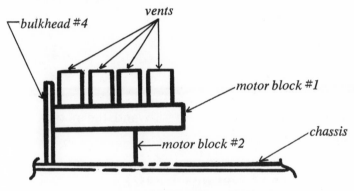

vents

—bulkhead #4

motor block #1

chassis

←motor block #2

Engine Assembly

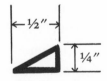

Tail Pipe Support
Make 2 from
rigid cardboard.
Paint black.

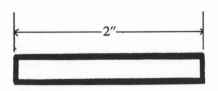

—2"—

Tail Pipe
Make 2 from large drinking straw.
Paint with aluminum paint.

When firmly attached, the pipes should point upward and back at a sharp angle; see diagram 15 and the photos of the finished model.

Engine Cylinders (Diagrams 15-16)

To give the engine of your Lotus-Ford racer a more realistic look, you may add several cylinders of different sizes. These are made of construction paper or large-size drinking straws. The model in the photos has four extra cylinders. See diagrams 15 and 16 for the sizes to draw and cut.

Cylinder #1 is made of any color construction paper you wish. It is ¾ inch long and when rolled into a cylinder has a diameter of ⅜ inch. Using different colored construction paper, cover both ends with ⅜-inch diameter discs (see diagram 15). The completed cylinder is attached in a horizontal position to the tail end of the chassis between the tail pipes.

176

DIAGRAM 15

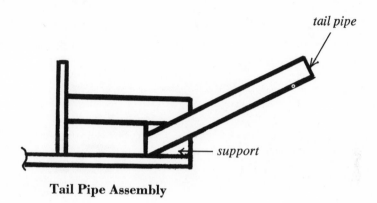

tail pipe

— *support*

Tail Pipe Assembly

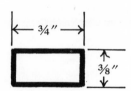

← ¾″ →

↕ ⅜″

Cylinder #1
Make 1 from
construction paper.

Wrap paper around pencil
and glue overlapping ends.

diameter

← ⅜″ →

Cylinder #1 Disc
Make 2 from
construction paper.

Glue to open ends
of cylinder #1.

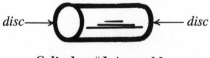

disc→   ←*disc*

Cylinder #1 Assembly

Cylinder #2
Make 1 from large
drinking straw.

Cylinders #3 and #4
Make 2 from large
drinking straw.

diameter

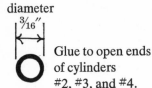

Glue to open ends
of cylinders
#2, #3, and #4.

Disc
Make 6 from
construction paper.

disc ——→   ←—— *disc*

Cylinder Assembly

Cylinder #2 is made from a ⅜-inch length of drinking straw with construction paper discs attached to both ends (see diagram 16). This is glued in an upright position on the tail end of motor block #2.

Cylinder #3 is made from a ½-inch length of drinking straw with construction paper discs covering both ends (see diagram 16). Glue it to the back of bulkhead #4 on the left, in the corner formed by motor blocks #1 and #2. This cylinder is attached in a vertical position.

Cylinder #4 is also made from a ½-inch length of drinking straw with construction paper discs on the ends (see diagram 16). Glue it in the right-hand corner across from cylinder #3. Attach one end of the cylinder to the back of bulkhead #4 so that the cylinder is in a horizontal position.

The cylinders made of drinking straws may be painted with any color poster paint you wish.

With the four engine cylinders in place, your Lotus-Ford Grand Prix racing model is complete.

178

McLaren M16: 1971

Peter Revson, a top American racing-car driver, waits in his McLaren racer for the start of the Indy 500 of 1971. INDIANAPOLIS MOTOR SPEEDWAY OFFICIAL PHOTO

Bruce McLaren, a native of New Zealand, blazed a brilliant racing record on tracks the world over. In 1960 McLaren placed second in the world competition for the best racing driver in Formula 1 contests. This is another term for Grand Prix competition, considered the supreme international class in automobile racing.

McLaren won the famous and long-established 24-hour Le Mans race in 1966. He took part in and won numerous Can-Am Races (Canadian-American Challenge Cup Races). What made McLaren's successes in this competition so outstanding

179

was the fact that several of his victories were achieved with cars that he himself had designed and built. Unlike Formula 1 racers, the Can-Am cars had no restrictions with regard to engine power, overall body design, or tires and wheels, among other features. From a standing position McLaren's Can-Am racers could streak to 100 miles per hour and slam to a stop again in the unbelievable time of less than 10 seconds. On straightaways his racers could easily reach the blistering pace of 200 miles per hour.

The Can-Am model was one type of successful racer McLaren created. Another equally successful type was his Formula 1 or Grand Prix racer, like the M16. It was also designed to participate in Indianapolis 500 races. This car had to be built within certain limitations of engine power, size, and weight, along with other requirements.

The McLaren M16 had a wedge-shaped body with its engine mounted in the rear. Above and behind the engine was an air foil, a structure rather like an airplane wing. Its purpose was to help hold the racer more firmly to the road while it moved at top speed. The foil was designed to work in an opposite way to an airplane wing which, when air flows over its upper and lower surfaces, creates a force that lifts the aircraft from the ground. Short stubby wings were also attached to each side of the racer's wedge-like nose and served the same purpose as the large rear-mounted air foil.

But air foils were not the only feature that gave the McLaren racer a different look. It also had enormously broad tires, almost 18 inches across. These huge tires gave the racer better traction, especially when the driver boomed into a curve.

The McLaren M16 could easily reach 200 miles per hour on straight stretches. In 1971 Peter Revson, a top American racing-car driver, guided one of McLaren's specialties to second-place position in the Indianapolis 500. The following year, in the same annual racing competition, Mark Donohue, an-

other superb American driver, brought a variation of one of McLaren's M16s home to victory.

Bruce McLaren gave his life to the sport of automobile racing on June 2, 1970. In the course of test driving one of his racing machines at Goodwood, England, he was killed instantly in an accident.

The M16, like all the McLaren cars, was an excellent racer, and it makes a handsome model.

BUILDING THE McLAREN M16 MODEL

Chassis (Diagram 1)

The chassis of the McLaren M16 model is made from rigid cardboard. Draw and cut it as shown in diagram 1. Since both ends of the chassis are almost identical, it will be helpful for construction of the model if one end is marked "front" and the other end "rear."

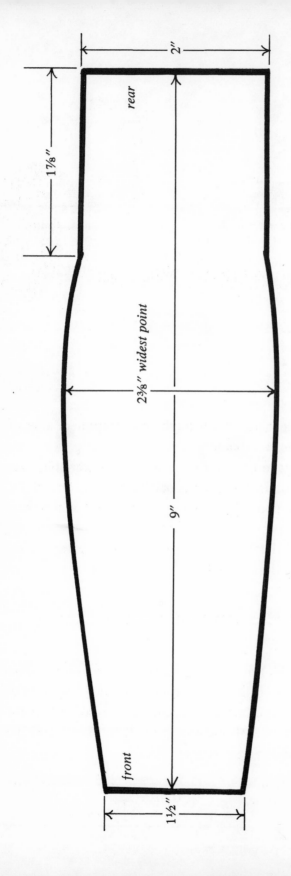

DIAGRAM 1

Chassis
Make 1 from rigid cardboard.

Note: This diagram is not to scale. Draw the chassis to the measurements given.

Bulkheads (Diagrams 2-3)

In order to give the proper shape to the body of the M16, and to have something on which to glue the body covering, a series of bulkheads is needed. These are made of rigid cardboard and glued at various points along the top side of the chassis. There are five bulkheads in all. Draw and cut them as shown in diagrams 2 and 3. Diagram 3 shows where to locate and glue each bulkhead on the chassis. Be sure to glue each bulkhead as perfectly upright as possible. If any of them slants, you will have difficulty attaching the body covering.

Nose Covering (Diagram 4)

The nose covering of the M16 is made in one piece from construction paper. Choose any color you wish. Draw and cut the covering as shown in diagram 4. Remember to draw the series of three parallel lines on each side of the nose before folding. Also remember to score the dotted lines with the point of your knife before folding. Scoring will give you straighter folds.

Begin attaching the nose covering by putting glue on the underside of the front edge. Press this to the front end of the chassis. Put glue along the top edges of bulkheads #1 and #2, and press the covering along these sections. You will notice that the nose covering slants sharply forward. Also, there is a slight overhang on bulkhead #2.

When the top sections are firmly attached, glue one side of the covering to the side edges of bulkheads #1 and #2; then glue the other side the same way. Finally, glue the gluing tabs (marked T) of the nose covering to the underside of the chassis.

Side Covering (Diagram 4)

Two pieces are needed to cover the sides of the M16. Draw and cut these pieces as shown in diagram 4. Use the same color construction paper you used for the nose covering. As you see, the side pieces taper from back to front.

DIAGRAM 2

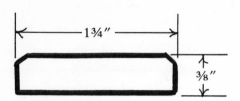

Bulkhead #1
Make 1 from
rigid cardboard.

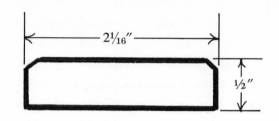

Bulkhead #2
Make 1 from
rigid cardboard.

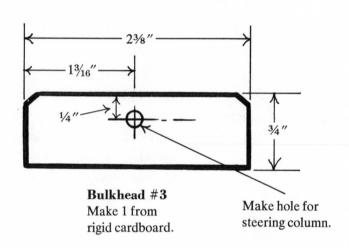

Bulkhead #3
Make 1 from
rigid cardboard.

Make hole for
steering column.

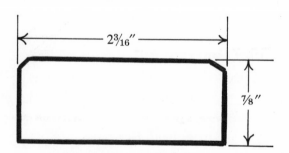

Bulkhead #4
Make 1 from rigid cardboard.

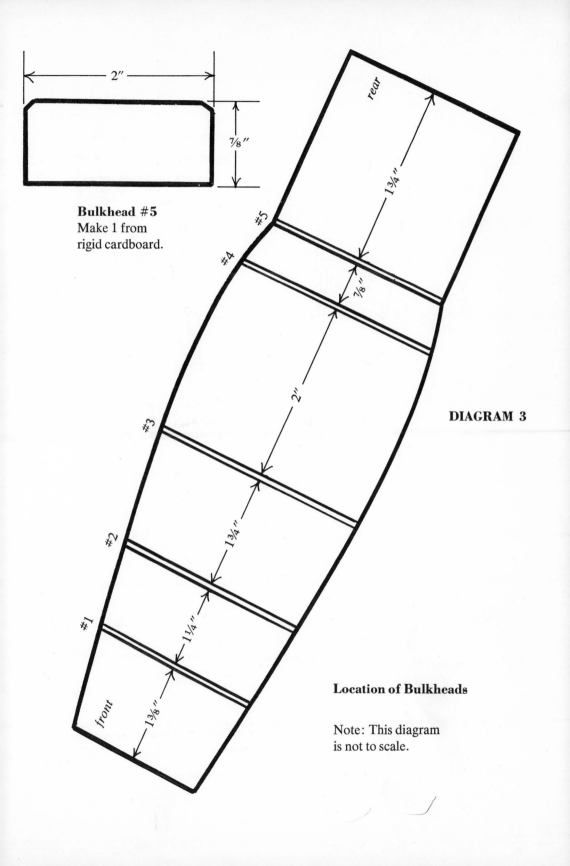

2″

7/8″

Bulkhead #5
Make 1 from
rigid cardboard.

rear

1 3/4″

#5

#4

7/8″

2″

#3

1 3/4″

#2

1 1/4″

#1

front

1 3/8″

DIAGRAM 3

Location of Bulkheads

Note: This diagram
is not to scale.

DIAGRAM 4

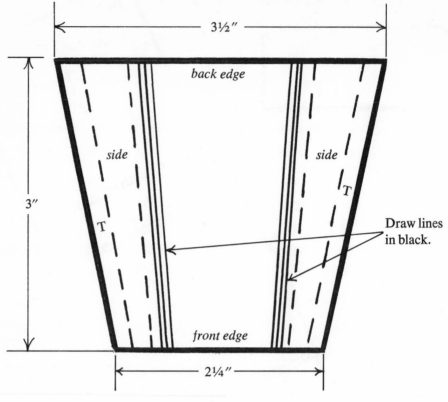

3½"

back edge

side   side

3"   T

T   Draw lines
                                         in black.

front edge

2¼"

Nose Covering

Make 1 from construction paper.

Fold on dotted lines.

Gluing tabs T are ¼" wide.
Fold them under chassis and glue.

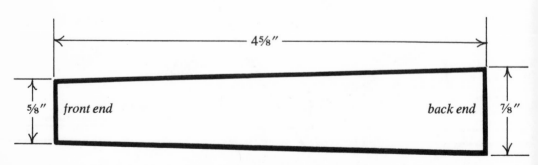

4⅝"

5⁄8"   front end   back end   7⁄8"

Side Covering
Make 2 from construction paper.

Put glue on the back and front ends of one side covering and along the bottom edge. Press the back end of the side covering to the edge of bulkhead #5. Then run your finger along the bottom edge, pressing firmly as you go, to attach it to the edge of the chassis. Finally, press the forward end of the side piece to the side edge of bulkhead #2.

After attaching one side covering, glue the other one to the other side of the racer, following the same procedure.

Driver's Compartment Covering (Diagram 5)

The driver's compartment covering is a little more complicated than what has been done so far. Draw and cut the covering as shown in diagram 5. Again, use the same color construction paper you used for the other pieces of body covering.

The covering is attached to bulkheads #2, #3, #4, and #5. Before gluing it around the driver's compartment, put it in place to check that it fits evenly at sides, back, and front. If there is any excess paper at these points, trim it with your scissors.

When you are satisfied that the covering fits properly, put a generous amount of glue on all four edges of the underside of the covering and press into position. Keep running your finger along the edges until they are firmly glued.

Before completing the body covering with the cockpit cowling, you will install the small parts in the driver's compartment.

Driver's Seat (Diagram 5)

Make and install the seat as the first of the pieces of equipment for the driver's compartment. Draw and cut the seat as shown in diagram 5. Use any color construction paper you wish. Fold the seat as shown in the diagram and glue it in place against bulkhead #5.

Gauges (Diagram 6)

Two small gauges and one large one are made from black construction paper and glued to the dashboard (the driver's side of

187

DIAGRAM 5

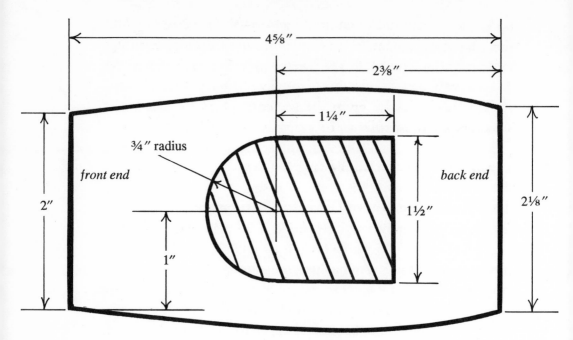

Driver's Compartment Covering
Make 1 from construction paper.

Cut out shaded portion.

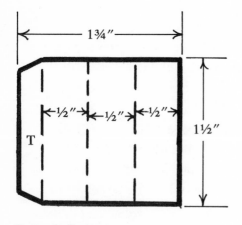

Driver's Seat
Make 1 from construction paper.

Gluing tab T is ¼″ wide.

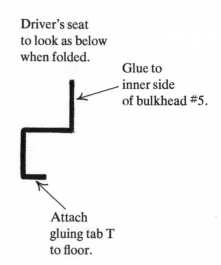

Driver's seat
to look as below
when folded.

Glue to
inner side
of bulkhead #5.

Attach
gluing tab T
to floor.

bulkhead #3). The gauges are positioned and glued near the top edge of the dashboard. The two small gauges are glued side by side at the left; the large gauge is glued at the upper right. Diagram 6 shows the sizes and shapes of the gauges. Diagram 7 shows their location on the dashboard. You will find that tweezers are most helpful for gluing these small pieces.

Brake and Gas Pedals (Diagram 6)

Two foot pedals, one large and one small, are installed in the driver's compartment. The larger pedal is the brake; the smaller one is the gas pedal. Both are made from rigid cardboard and painted black with India ink or poster paint. See diagram 6 for the sizes and shapes to be drawn and cut.

Attach the pedals at a slant at the bottom of the dashboard, ¼ inch apart. The ends of the pedals are glued to the dashboard and to the floor of the driver's compartment. Locate the pedals approximately in the center of the dashboard at equal distances from the sides of the driver's compartment. See diagram 7 for placement.

Steering Wheel (Diagram 6)

The steering unit consists of a steering column and a steering wheel. The steering column is made from a 2-inch length of a large wooden matchstick (see diagram 6).

The steering wheel is made from rigid cardboard. Use your compass to draw a circle with ⅝-inch diameter (see diagram 6). Press quite firmly on your compass as you go over the circle again and again. This will make an indentation in the cardboard and help you cut a more perfect circle. Remember to turn the piece continuously into your scissors while cutting. Draw the wheel rim and spokes on one side of the wheel with red ink, poster paint, or crayon.

Glue the wheel to the steering column (see diagram 6). Be sure that the end of the column is in the center of the wheel. When both are firmly joined, put a generous amount of glue on

DIAGRAM 6

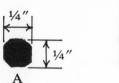

A

B

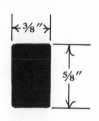

Brake Pedal

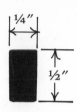

Gas Pedal

Gauges
Make 2 of gauge A and 1 of gauge B
from black construction paper.

Make 1 of each pedal
from rigid cardboard.
Paint black.

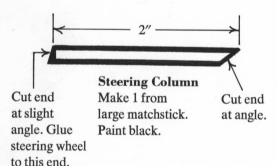

Steering Column
Make 1 from
large matchstick.
Paint black.

Cut end
at slight
angle. Glue
steering wheel
to this end.

Cut end
at angle.

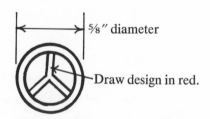

⅝″ diameter

Draw design in red.

Steering Wheel
Make 1 from
rigid cardboard.

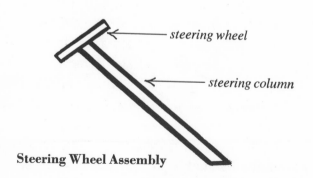

steering wheel

steering column

Steering Wheel Assembly

DIAGRAM 7

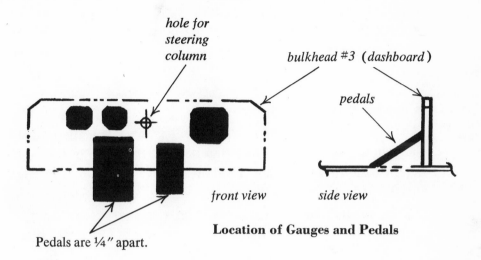

hole for
steering
column

bulkhead #3 (dashboard)

pedals

front view   side view

Location of Gauges and Pedals

Pedals are ¼" apart.

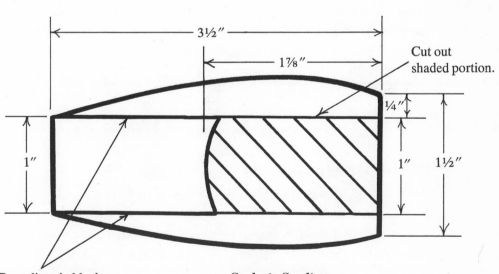

3½"

1⅞"

Cut out
shaded portion.

¼"

1"

1"   1½"

Draw lines in black.
Fold on these lines before gluing.

Cockpit Cowling
Make 1 from construction paper.

the opposite end of the steering column and push it through the hole in the dashboard. When you feel the end of the column touch the floor of the chassis, hold it in position for the few moments until the glue sets. Finally, put a generous amount of glue at the point where the steering column enters the hole in the dashboard; this will make a firm attachment for the steering assembly.

Cockpit Cowling (Diagram 7)

The cowling around the driver's compartment is a streamlined portion of the body covering that deflects the force of the wind against the driver at high speed. It is attached to the top edge of the driver's compartment. Draw and cut the cowling as shown in diagram 7. Again, use the same color construction paper as the other sections of body covering. Draw the black lines as shown in the diagram and fold the cowling as indicated.

To attach the cowling, put a generous amount of glue along its under edges. Position the front part of the cowling about $3\frac{1}{4}$ inches from the front end of the racer's body. Press it down firmly. Then very carefully press the side edges in place. Before the glue hardens along these side edges, make certain that the folded lines slant upward and do not lie flat against the car's body. Finally, glue the two tail ends of the cowling at the back edge of the driver's compartment. These two ends are glued flat. The finished cowling should have a somewhat twisted, angular form. See the photos on pages 181, 201, and 215.

Windshield (Diagram 8)

The windshield is made of white construction paper. It is glued around the top edge of the cowling, surrounding the driver.

The author found it easier to make the windshield in three pieces rather than a single piece because of the complex curves to which it is shaped. However, you may be successful in making it of one piece. Try experimenting; if it doesn't work, make three separate pieces and attach them as explained below.

DIAGRAM 8

Windshield

Part #1
Make 1 from white
construction paper.

Draw these lines in
2 places in black.

Glue part #2 at dotted line;
trim as needed.

1¼″ radius

1½″ radius

Draw circular outlines
with compass in
two positions.

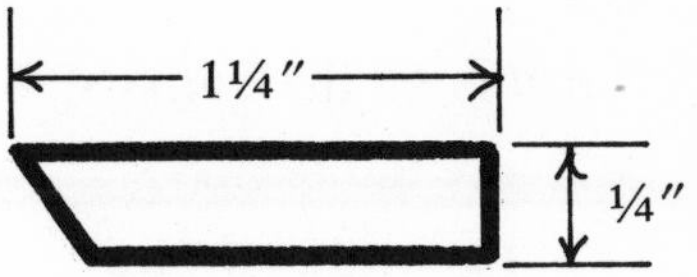

|← 1¼″ →|

¼″

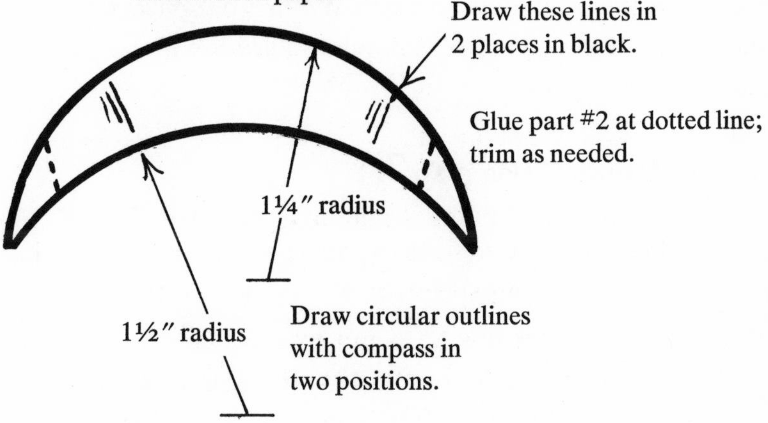

Part #2
Make 2 from white
construction paper.

part #1

part #2

part #2

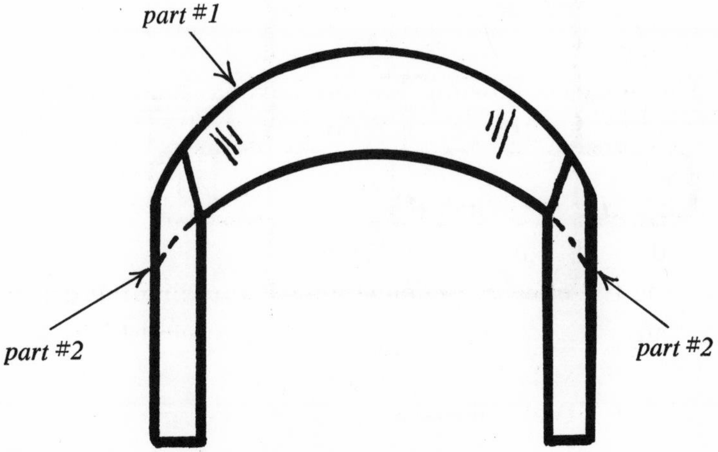

Windshield Assembly

Draw and cut the three windshield parts as shown in diagram 8. Part #1 is the main, front portion. Part #2 is the side portion; make two of these and glue them to part #1 as shown in diagram 8. After the windshield is assembled, glue it around the inner edge of the cowling. This will require patience since you will have to hold the windshield in place a section at a time until the glue hardens.

Rear Axle Mount (Diagram 9)

The McLaren M16 racer has a rear axle mount made of any color construction paper you wish. Draw and cut it as shown in diagram 9.

After the axle mount has been put together as shown in the diagram, glue it to the chassis. Position the axle mount ⅛ inch in from the rear end of the chassis and ³⁄₁₆ inch in from each side. Put lots of glue on the bottom side of the mount and press it firmly to the chassis.

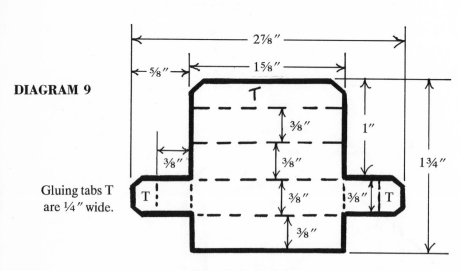

DIAGRAM 9

Gluing tabs T are ¼" wide.

Rear Axle Mount
Make 1 from construction paper.
Fold on dotted lines.

Rear axle mount
to look as at right
when folded and glued.

DIAGRAM 10

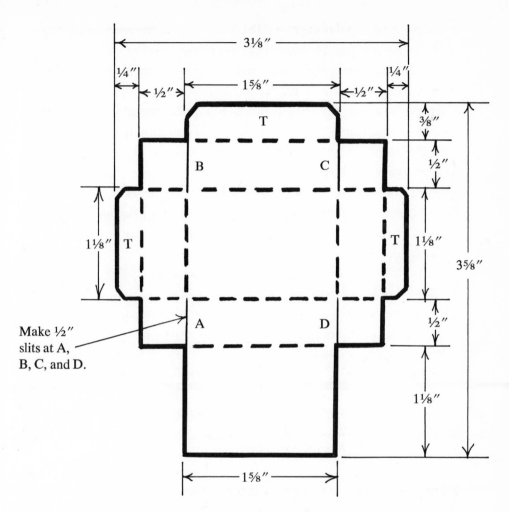

Make ½″ slits at A, B, C, and D.

Engine Block
Make 1 from construction paper.

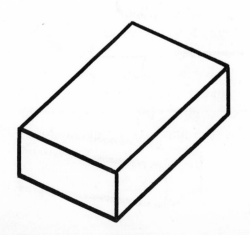

Engine block to look as at left when folded and glued.

Engine Block (Diagram 10)

The engine of the McLaren M16 model consists of two rectangular units (engine block and engine head), two exhaust systems, eight engine vents, an air filter, and a coil.

Draw and cut the engine block from construction paper as shown in diagram 10. Use any color paper you wish. Fold and glue the engine block according to the diagram. Glue it to the chassis between bulkhead #5 and the rear axle mount. The ends of the engine block will barely touch the bulkhead and axle mount. The short sides of the engine block should parallel the side edges of the chassis, about ¼ inch in from each side edge.

Engine Head (Diagram 11)

The engine head is another rectangular unit made from construction paper. Choose a different color from that of the engine block. Draw and cut the engine head as shown in diagram 11. Assemble the engine head according to the diagram. Then glue it to the top of the engine block. Position the engine head so its short sides face back and front. The back end of the engine head will extend over the rear axle mount. See the photos of the finished model for placement (pages 181, 201, and 215).

Exhaust System (Diagram 12)

The exhaust system of the McLaren model has two units—one for the left side of the engine and one for the right side. Both units are exactly alike and are made from lengths of drinking straws. Each unit is made up of one 2-inch long pipe piece and four pieces—vents—¼ inch long. The ¼-inch vents are glued to the 2-inch pipe about ¼ inch apart, starting even with one end of the pipe. See diagram 12 for assembling these parts.

After completing the two exhaust units, attach them to the right and left of the engine head by gluing the small vents to the sides of the engine head. Make sure that one end of the 2-inch

196

DIAGRAM 11

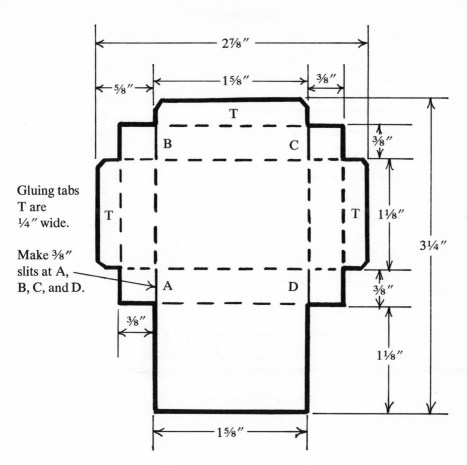

Engine Head
Make 1 from construction paper.

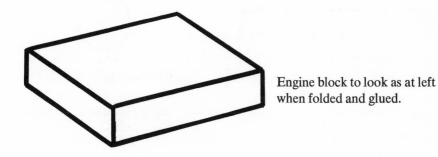

Engine block to look as at left
when folded and glued.

DIAGRAM 12

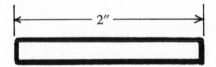

Exhaust Pipe
Make 2 from drinking straw.

Exhaust Vent
Make 8 from
drinking straw.

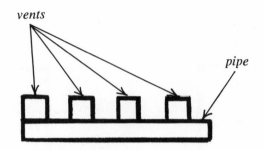

Exhaust System Assembly

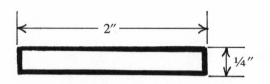

Air Filter Body
Make 1 from
construction paper.

Roll air filter body into ring.

pipe presses against and is glued to bulkhead #5. The other end will extend rearward beyond the engine head. See the photo of the finished model on page 201 for placement.

Air Filter (Diagrams 12-13)

The air filter is a ring ½ inch in diameter. Make it from bright-colored construction paper, such as red.

Cut the paper in a strip ¼ inch wide and about 2 inches long (see diagram 12). Roll the strip around a thick pencil, rod, or even your finger to make a ring about ½ inch in diameter. Check this with your ruler. When you are satisfied, glue the ends of the strip together. Press the ends firmly until you are sure they will hold.

Next, draw and cut a ⅝-inch diameter cap from different colored construction paper, as shown in diagram 13. The cap is slightly larger in diameter than the ring, so it will hang over the edge all around. Remember to use your compass repeatedly over the circle to form a deep indentation. This will help you to cut the cap into a nearly perfect circle. Glue the cap to one end of the air filter ring. Then glue the completed air filter to the top center of the engine head. See the photo of the finished model on page 201 for placement.

Coil (Diagram 13)

The coil is an electrical device necessary for starting the Mc-Laren's engine. It is made of construction paper, a bright color different from the air filter.

Draw and cut a strip of construction paper to the size shown in diagram 13. Shape it into a ring by first forming it around a pencil or rod. When the ring has a diameter of ⅜ inch, glue the overlapping ends together. Press the ends to make sure they are firmly attached.

Next, close the openings of the ring with two discs ⅜ inch in diameter (see diagram 13). These are made of the same

DIAGRAM 13

diameter

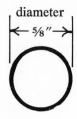

Air Filter Cap
Make 1 from
construction paper.

cap

body

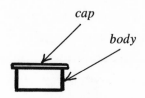

Air Filter Assembly

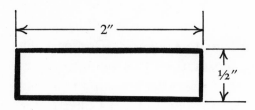

Coil Body
Make 1 from
construction paper.

diameter
⅜″

Roll coil body
into ring.

diameter
⅜″

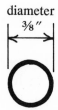

Coil Disc
Make 2 from
construction paper.

body

disc   disc

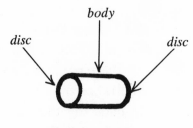

Coil Assembly

color construction paper as the body of the coil. Use your compass in the same way you did for the air filter cap in order to cut the best possible circles.

After completing the coil, glue it to the back end of the engine head, overhanging the axle mount. The coil is attached along its ½-inch side. When it is installed, the engine of your McLaren M16 will be complete.

Air Scoops (Diagram 14)

Two air scoops are needed for the McLaren M16—one for the right side of the body and one for the left side. The scoops are made from the same color construction paper as the racer's body covering. Draw and cut the scoops as shown in diagram 14. Draw the black line design on the top of each scoop with India ink or black crayon (see diagram 14).

Fold and glue the air scoops to form the box shape shown in

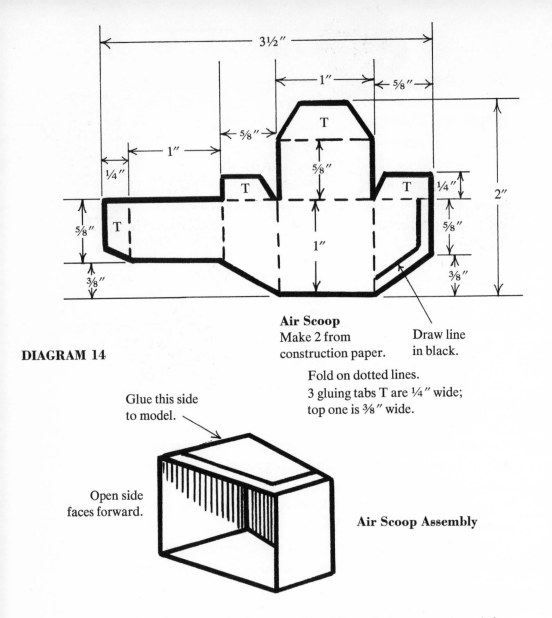

DIAGRAM 14

Air Scoop
Make 2 from
construction paper.

Draw line
in black.

Fold on dotted lines.
3 gluing tabs T are ¼" wide;
top one is ⅜" wide.

Glue this side
to model.

Open side
faces forward.

Air Scoop Assembly

the diagram. Attach them to the sides of the racer by gluing the long side of each scoop to the racer, with the closed back end even with the rear end of the body. See the photo of the finished model for placement.

Front Air Foils (Diagram 15)

Two air foils are needed for the front end of the McLaren M16.

202

Draw and cut these from rigid cardboard as shown in diagram 15. Paint both air foils with poster paint, any color you wish. Or you may cover them with colored construction paper; this is a bit more complicated than painting them.

After finishing the foils, glue one on the right side of the racer's nose and one on the left side. Glue each foil ⅜ inch in from the front edge of the racer and midway between the top and bottom of the nose. See the photo of the finished model for placement.

Rear Air Foil (Diagrams 15-16)

A rear-mounted air foil is used on many racing cars to help hold them to the ground at high speeds. The foil's design makes it work just the opposite of an airplane wing. Air currents flowing over an airplane wing produce a lifting force, while air currents flowing over the foil of a racing car create a downward pushing force.

On the McLaren racer, the rear air foil consists of the foil itself, four air flow guides, and a mounting bracket. Draw and cut the foil from rigid cardboard as shown in diagram 15. Paint the foil with poster paint or cover it with construction paper the way you did the front foils. Make the rear air foil the same color as the front ones.

Draw and cut the four air flow guides from any color construction paper you wish. See diagram 15 for their size and shape. One pair is glued to the underside of the foil, and the other pair is glued directly on top of the lower ones. They are located ¼ inch in from the ends of the foil; see diagram 15.

The bracket for mounting the rear air foil to the racer consists of two lengths of large wooden matchsticks and two short braces, also made from large matchsticks. See diagram 16 for the correct lengths of these pieces; cut the ends to the angles shown. Paint all four pieces black.

Glue the ends of the two long support brackets to the under-

DIAGRAM 15

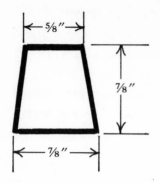

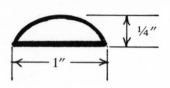

Front Air Foil
Make 2 from
rigid cardboard.

Air Flow Guide
Make 4 from
construction paper.

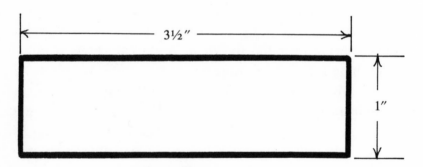

Rear Air Foil
Make 1 from
rigid cardboard.

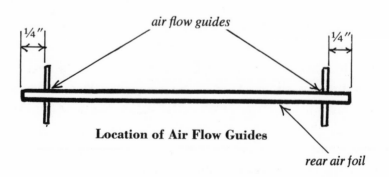

air flow guides

Location of Air Flow Guides

rear air foil

DIAGRAM 16

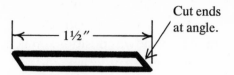

Cut ends at angle.

1½″

Long Support Bracket
Make 2 from large matchstick.
Paint black.

⅜″

Cut 1 end at angle.

Short Brace
Make 2 from large matchstick.
Paint black.

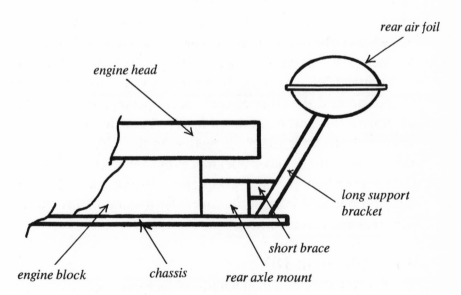

rear air foil

engine head

long support bracket

short brace

engine block   *chassis*   *rear axle mount*

Rear Air Foil Assembly

side of the rear air foil, 1 inch in from the ends of the foil and 1¼ inches apart. Hold each bracket in place until the glue hardens. It is best to do this with the foil resting on two supports in an upside-down position. When these brackets are firmly attached, glue their other ends to the rear end of the chassis. The brackets will slant upward to the rear. Hold the unit in place until the glue sets.

The foil and its brackets will not become really secure until the two short braces are added. These are glued near the bottom of each bracket, with the other end at the rear axle mount. See diagram 16 for placement.

Wheels (Diagram 17)

Each wheel and axle assembly of the McLaren M16 consists of a pair of wheels, wheel covers, an axle, and two axle supports.

The wheels are made from a cardboard cylinder from a roll of paper toweling. Two front wheels are cut to a width of ⅞ inch; two rear wheels are cut to a width of 1 inch. The openings of all four wheels are covered with discs of white construction paper. All eight discs are the same diameter as the wheels. Draw the tire and wheel design on one side of each disc with India ink or black poster paint. See diagram 17 for the sizes and designs.

To attach the covers to the wheels, put a generous amount of glue around the edge of the wheel opening. Place a wheel cover over this and press down firmly. Turn the wheel upside-down with the attached cover resting on the table and glue the second cover to the other opening. Press down firmly. Put your ruler across the top of the wheel and a weight (such as a scissors or a bottle of ink) on the ruler; let it stand undisturbed as you work on another wheel.

Axles (Diagram 18)

The two axles are 5¾-inch lengths of large wooden matchsticks (see diagram 18). Paint the axles black with India ink or poster paint.

DIAGRAM 17

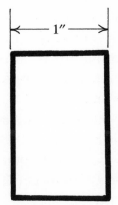

Front Wheel
Make 2 from
cardboard cylinder.
Paint outside black.

Rear Wheel
Make 2 from
cardboard cylinder.
Paint outside black.

Wheel Cover
Make 8 from white construction paper.

Diameter of cover is same as wheel diameter.

Draw design on 1 side in black.

Wheel and Axle Assembly

Attach the front wheels to an axle first. To do this, punch a small hole in the exact center of one cover of a front wheel. This will become the inner side of the wheel (the side facing the car). Use a sharp pointed tool such as a nail to make the hole. If it is not large enough for the axle to fit through, enlarge it by twirling the point of your pencil in it. Be careful not to make the hole too large, or the axle and wheel will not glue together securely.

Next, put a generous amount of glue on one end of the axle. Push this end through the hole until you feel the inside of the opposite cover (the outer one). Hold the axle and wheel at right angles to one another as straight as possible. It is best to do this with the wheel resting flat on your work surface and the axle pointing straight up.

While the glue is hardening on the first wheel, make two holes in the sides of the racer's body, one on the left and one on the right, directly opposite one another. See diagram 18 for the exact location of these holes. They must be large enough for the axle to slip through. It is very important to make them exactly in line with one another or the wheels will be crooked and will spoil the appearance of your finished model.

Push the axle with one wheel attached through the holes. Attach the second wheel as you did the first. Begin by making a hole for the axle in the inner wheel cover.

When the second wheel is firmly glued, check to see that the wheels are an equal distance from the sides of the racer's body. You can move the axle right or left to adjust this. When they look right, put a generous amount of glue at the points where the axle enters the car's body. After the glue hardens, the wheel and axle will be firmly locked in position.

The rear wheels are both glued to the axle at the same time, since the rear axle will be glued to the exposed axle mount. Attach the rear wheels to the axle the same way you attached

DIAGRAM 18

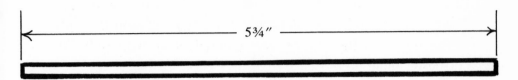

Axle
Make 2 from large matchstick. Paint black.

Note: This diagram is not to scale. Cut axles to measurement given.

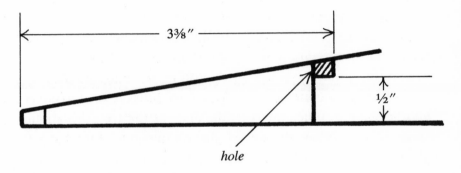

Location of Holes for Front Axle

the front wheels. When they are firmly glued, place a generous amount of glue on the top surface of the axle mount. Slide the wheel and axle assembly onto it. If necessary, move the wheels to right or left until they are equally spaced from the sides of the racer and exactly in line with the front wheels. Then put the model on a support with the wheels off the table until both front and rear wheel assemblies are firmly attached.

Axle Supports (Diagram 19)

In the meantime, cut four axle supports from a large wooden matchstick. These will strengthen the wheel and axle assemblies. The two front supports are 7/8 inch long; the two rear supports are 1¼ inches long. See diagram 19 for the angles at the ends. Like the axles, the supports are painted black with India ink or poster paint.

The front supports are glued at an angle from the racer's sides to the axle where it touches the wheel (see diagram 19). The rear supports are glued from the sides of the engine block to the axle (see diagram 19). The photos on pages 201 and 215 show the placement of the axle supports.

Roll Bar (Diagram 20)

The roll bar of the McLaren M16 is made from a 2-inch length of pipe cleaner and painted with aluminum paint after it has been bent. See diagram 20 for the shape to bend the bar.

The roll bar is mounted on the top of the body directly behind the driver's compartment. Make two holes in the top covering the same distance apart as the ends of the bar; this should be about 1¼ inches. Put lots of glue on the ends of the bar and push each end into a hole. Make sure the bar does not tilt to one side or the other. See the photos of the finished model for placement.

Rear View Mirror (Diagram 20)

The rear view mirror assembly consists of the mirror and four pieces for a mounting bracket. Draw and cut the mirror from rigid cardboard as shown in diagram 20. Paint one side with aluminum paint. This side will represent the mirror.

The four pieces of the mounting bracket are made from round toothpicks. Cut them to the correct length and shapes as shown in diagram 20, and paint them black.

The bracket pieces are glued to form a tripod. Start assem-

DIAGRAM 19

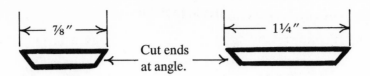

⟵ ⅞″ ⟶   Cut ends   ⟵ 1¼″ ⟶
            at angle.

Front Axle Support
Make 2 from
large matchstick.
Paint black.

Rear Axle Support
Make 2 from
large matchstick.
Paint black.

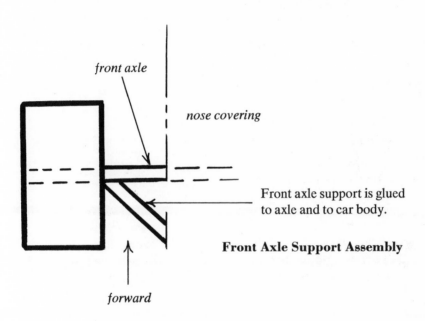

front axle

nose covering

Front axle support is glued
to axle and to car body.

Front Axle Support Assembly

forward

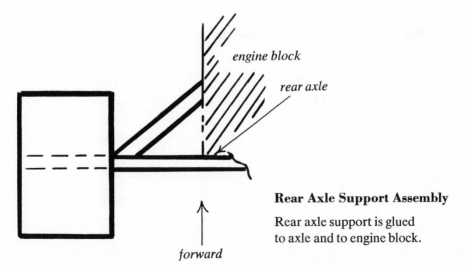

engine block

rear axle

Rear Axle Support Assembly

Rear axle support is glued
to axle and to engine block.

forward

DIAGRAM 20

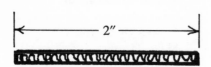

Roll Bar
Make 1 from pipe cleaner.

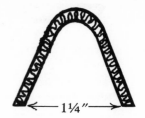

Bend roll bar as above.
Paint with aluminum paint.

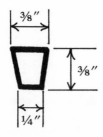

Rear View Mirror
Make 1 from rigid cardboard.
Paint with aluminum paint.

Cut
one end
at angle.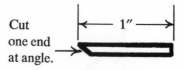

**Mirror Bracket
Parts A and B**
Make 2 from
round toothpick.
Paint black.

Cut
one end
at angle. →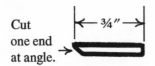

**Mirror Bracket
Part C**
Make 1 from
round toothpick.
Paint black.

**Mirror Bracket
Part D**
Make 1 from
round toothpick.
Paint black.

bling the bracket by gluing the 1-inch lengths (A and B) together in an angle (see diagram 21). Glue part C—¾ inch long—to the point of the angle, for the third leg of the tripod (see diagram 21). Part D, the fourth and shortest piece of the bracket—⅜ inch long—is first glued to the back of the mirror and then to the top point of the bracket, where the tripod comes together. You may have some difficulty holding the mirror straight until the glue hardens, but it can be done; just be patient.

When the bracket and mirror are assembled, glue the unit to the racer. It is located on the left side of the body, almost even with the front edge of the driver's compartment. Two legs of the bracket are glued to the side of the body and the third shorter leg on top of the cowling. See the photos on pages 201 and 215 for correct placement.

Number (Diagram 21)

The identification number of the McLaren M16 consists of a white disc and a black number. Draw and cut the disc from white construction paper, as shown in diagram 21. The number may be drawn directly on the disc with India ink or cut from black construction paper. Follow the pattern in diagram 21 or select any other number you wish.

The disc with its number is glued on the top of the nose section about 1⅛ inches from the edge of the driver's compartment.

Trim (Diagram 21)

The trim for the racer's front edge is the last item to be added to your model. Draw and cut the trim as shown in diagram 21. Use a different color construction paper from the body of the racer.

Fold the trim along the dotted line. Then position and glue length A-B across the front of the racer, matching the fold with the front edge.

DIAGRAM 21

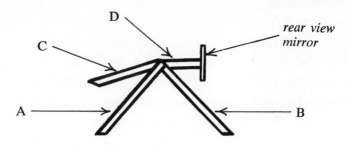

Rear View Mirror Assembly

diameter
1"

Draw number in black
or cut from black
construction paper.

Number
Make 1 disc from
white construction paper.

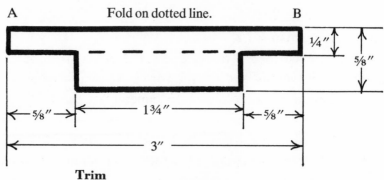

Fold on dotted line.

Trim
Make 1 from construction paper.

Bend under the overhanging ends A and B and glue them under the nose. Then glue the folded section of the trim to the front of the racer. See the photo of the finished model.

This completes your McLaren M16 racer. If you have made all the models with care, you will have an attractive fleet representing more than seventy years of automobile racing.

Glossary

Air Scoop: This is a large, pan-shaped unit that filters the air sucked into a running engine. It helps to reduce engine wear.

Bulkheads: These are vertical sections fixed at various points on the chassis. They provide attachment points for the body covering, giving it form and strength. Bulkheads are important structural pieces on real racing cars as well as models.

Chassis: This is the basic frame of an automobile to which the wheels, engine, and body are attached.

Cowling: This is part of the body covering of a racing car that extends around the upper part of the driver's cockpit. Its purpose is to deflect the wind from the driver while the car is moving at high speed.

Dashboard: The panel directly in front of the driver's cockpit is called the dashboard. Various gauges are attached to it that give a driver information on such things as speed, oil pressure, and engine temperature.

Formula 1: This designates the specifications for the kind of car used in Grand Prix races. In general this is a small racer with its engine in the rear; it has room for only one person, the driver; it has an open cockpit; and there are no fenders over its wheels. On straightaways the low-slung racer can reach a top speed of close to 200 miles per hour.

Gear Shift: This is a lever for changing the relationship of gears in the transmission housing. Gear changes are usually made in conjunction with acceleration to make a racer go faster or slower, or to go into reverse.

Grand Prix: These are French words meaning "big prize." The term designates a series of international auto road races that are ranked as the world's greatest. At the end of the Grand

216

Prix season, in which there may be as many as 12 competitions, the driver with the most victories receives the coveted award, World Championship of Drivers.

Lap: A lap is one complete turn around a racecourse or track.

Leaf Spring: This is a long, horizontal spring made up of layers of separate metal sections or leaves of various lengths.

Roll Bar: This is a loop-shaped steel frame extending above and to the back of the driver's head. The bar is a safety device to prevent the driver from being crushed in roll-over accidents.

Sprocket Chain: On many early cars, especially the racers, the engine power was transmitted to the rear wheels by means of a sprocket gear and chain, similar to the arrangement on a bicycle. The drive shaft, universal on today's cars, came into popular use during the first decade of the 1900s.

Steering Lever: The first automobiles had steering levers, or tillers, instead of wheels.

Further Reading

Borgenson, Griffith. *The Golden Age of the American Racing Car*. New York: W. W. Norton and Company, Inc., 1966.

Dymock, Eric. *The World of Racing Cars*. London–New York: The Hamlyn Publishing Group Limited, 1972.

Purdy, Ken W. *The Kings of the Road*. Boston: Little, Brown and Company, 1949.

Radosta, John S. *The New York Times Complete Guide to Auto Racing*. Chicago: Quadrangle Books, Inc., 1971.

Stanley, Louis T. *Grand Prix 10*. New York: David McKay Company, Inc., 1969.

Index

*indicates photo

ABOUT THE AUTHOR

Frank Ross, Jr., is the author of some forty books for young people. His enthusiasm for scientific and technological subjects is conveyed in his clearly written and exciting books on such topics as weather, transportation, automobile racing, and aircraft, as well as several other fascinating books on models and how to make them.

Mr. Ross lives in Southampton, New York, with his wife Laura Ross, who is also an author of books for young people.